The Earthwise Home Manual

The Earthwise Home Manual

ECO-FRIENDLY INTERIOR DESIGN AND HOME IMPROVEMENT

Kristina Diana Detjen

Green Home Publishing

Cover design and illustration: Stewart Hartsfield
Page design and layout: Another Jones Graphics

Detjen, Kristina.
   The earthwise home manual : eco-friendly interior
decorating and home improvement / by Kristina Detjen.
   p. cm.
   Includes bibliographical references and index.
   ISBN 0-9768369-0-4

   1. Interior decoration--Health aspects.   I. Title.

NK2113.D48 2006   613'.5
                QB105-600134

ISBN 10: 0-9768369-0-4
ISBN 13: 978-0-9768369-0-2

Printed in the USA

This book is printed on recycled paper.
Ten percent of the proceeds from the sales of this book
will be donated to environmental causes.

This book is dedicated
to preserving our magnificent Earth
for future generations!

TURN YOUR HOME INTO AN ECO-FRIENDLY JEWEL.

"The Human Soul needs Beauty more than Bread."

—D. H. Lawrence

Acknowledgements

I would like to thank all these people for their time, knowledge, and support.

Raymond Jester, Donya Wiland, Shannon Nelson, Ken Reilly, Bill Johnson, Tom Wilcox, Sabrina Park, Paul Edwards, Jim Newcomer, Sharon Patterson, Sanda Altman, Brandy Whyte, Josh Badden, Ernie Chapman, Ken Aust, Elizabeth Grossman, Jan Springer, Mark Pendleton, Ryan Temple, Lincoln Reed, Carolyn Barnard, Donald Altman, Shannon Nelson, Brooke Monfort, Stewart Hartsfield, Anita Jones, Heidi Creson and Raphael Cushnir.

CONTENTS

Chapter 5: The Bedroom - Sleep Soundly and Wake Up

Introduction

ECO-FRIENDLY INTERIOR DESIGN
& HOME IMPROVEMENT

AN IDEA
WHOSE TIME HAS COME

"We seek a renewed stirring for life on Earth.
We plead of what we are capable of doing is
not always what we ought to do.
We urge that all people now determine
that a wide untrammeled freedom shall remain
to testify that this generation has love for the next."
—Nancy Newhall

Home is where your life is. That is where we sleep, dream, eat and live. That is where we wake, get ready for work, and where we return each evening. It is our retreat when we are sick, where we keep our treasures, and bring our family and friends. It's no wonder that home is *the* most important place in our lives. We want home to be a place of great comfort, individuality and renewed inspiration. We also want our home to reflect our greatest values and place in the world. For those of us who care deeply about the Earth and do things like recycle cans and buy organic food to lesson our impact on the planet, we may want to extend that commitment to home improvement. By purchasing eco-friendly home products, we can make a positive impact on the world around us. Just consider this: The average American middle-class family uses four million pounds of the Earth's resources each year! Four million pounds![1] This is a mammoth quantity.

Is there a way our home improvements can help soften our "foot prints" on the Earth, while allowing us to fulfill our dreams of making our homes as beautiful and comfortable as possible? Yes, yes, and yes. Most people would be surprised to learn that they can purchase basic items like carpeting, cabinets and furniture that are eco-friendly and just as beautiful, luxurious, durable and economical as "standard" products. Most people would also delight in knowing that by being eco-friendly, they can save money by conserving energy with efficient household appliances, conserving water, and refinishing existing household items, rather than buying new ones. We can also increase our vitality by becoming aware of, and cutting back on sources of household pollutants such as VOC's (volatile organic compounds) and other damaging chemicals in paint and finishing products, carpeting, furniture, synthetic bedding and window fabrics, and in household cleaners. The list of eco-friendly household products is vast and can bring you gratification and financial savings. Environmental sustainability is a reality for those who take the time to learn about and pursue the possibilities. The path is golden, so why not take it?

◎ ◎ ◎ ◎ ◎ ◎ ◎ ◎ ◎ ◎ ◎ ◎ ◎

How it all began...

Did you ever have an epiphany or a sudden realization about something? Once I had an epiphany while searching for a house in Portland, Oregon. In fact, it inspired this book. One glorious summer afternoon, when the trees were green, lush and full, I was combing my favorite neighborhood searching for the house of my dreams, when I came upon a beautiful yellow 1920's traditional; complete with quaint cottage landscaping and giant elm trees in front. It was what I had always pictured as my ideal home. As I started to ascend wooden steps, a warm and friendly woman with long, silver-streaked hair and dressed in a colorful cotton peasant skirt, came out to greet me. 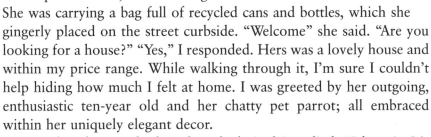 She was carrying a bag full of recycled cans and bottles, which she gingerly placed on the street curbside. "Welcome" she said. "Are you looking for a house?" "Yes," I responded. Hers was a lovely house and within my price range. While walking through it, I'm sure I couldn't help hiding how much I felt at home. I was greeted by her outgoing, enthusiastic ten-year old and her chatty pet parrot; all embraced within her uniquely elegant decor.

    "What do you think?" she asked. And I replied, "I love it. It's almost exactly what I am looking for." Hopeful, she asked if I wanted to buy it. I responded that I wouldn't be able to, because her house was already fixed up. As an interior designer, I wanted a house I could fix up myself—a house with holes in the floor, stains in the carpet and cabinet doors falling off their hinges. "I'm looking for something that desperately needs work," I told her. She expressed that it wasn't a problem since I could just tear everything down and start anew. I explained that my personal choices prevented me from that approach because it would be such a waste of resources. I watched her face droop in obvious embarrassment. Here was a person who clearly loved the Earth, but who, like scores of others, had not considered the link between recycling her cans and bottles and conserving the resources that went into making her own home. This encounter led to the following epiphany: Even though so many of us care passionately about the fate of the Earth, we are often completely unaware of how our own personal actions contribute to its very destruction. This is when my personal mission kicked in—to increase awareness by showing people how to decorate and improve their homes in an Earthwise, elegant and affordable way.

When people talk about getting an oriental rug that can be tossed later, as a temporary solution to a problem room, my eyes glaze over. Or when I hear someone talking about completely remodeling a kitchen, redone just five years ago, merely to change a color scheme, I feel disappointed and deeply sad. This is why I wrote this book: to show people how they can make their homes beautiful and functional while saving the Earth's resources.

What is the Definition of a Consumer? One who Consumes the Earth.

Now that I've dedicated over four years of my life to writing about environmental interior design and home improvement, I brainstorm about ways to make it more appealing and interesting. Maybe if there was a clever, simple, and fun way to explain the philosophy behind eco-friendly home design—in the form of a cartoon description, then more people would quickly adopt it. Ah ha, the noodle-haired monster who hungrily devours the Earth's resources. We all love cartoons so here it is. Think about this: "Industry moves, mines, shovels, burns, wastes, pumps and disposes of four million pounds of material in order to provide one, average American middle-class family's needs for a year," writes authors Paul Hawken and Amory and Hunter Lovins in *Natural Capitalism*.[2] They say that, "For all the world to live as an American or Canadian, we would need two more Earths to satisfy everyone."[3] This is a lot of stuff. If there is ever to be a sustainable balance on Earth, with enough resources for everyone, we will have to change our relationship to consumption and use far less.

According to the Wuppertal Institute of Germany, we will have to learn to live with fewer products and at a higher efficiency—*by a factor of ten!* That means that each person in an industrialized country who has an average daily resource diet of 115 pounds will have to cut back to a diet of 11.5 pounds![4]

Although these projections seem formidable, this goal is not impossible to achieve. For example, on this path to simplification, people in industrialized countries will have to learn to use one-tenth the energy for every warm night at home or one-tenth the amount of pesticide now used for every bale of cotton grown. It would also mean doing things like reupholstering or putting slip covers on an old sofa instead of taking it to the dump, or refinishing or repainting kitchen cabinets instead of cutting down trees for brand new ones. If we do things like invest more in energy research and manufacturing efficiency, and simply learn to live with less, we can achieve this goal. There may come a day when we no longer have a choice. Remember, think in factors of ten; if things are ever going to improve, we will have to do a whole lot more than recycle. And if you think you are too small to make an impact, think of a mosquito in someone's bed. The key to effecting things globally is in acting locally!

In terms of home improvement, we gobble up the Earth in the form of everyday home products like stone, gravel, fresh water, oil, natural gas, wood, metals, chemicals, plastics, textiles and rubber. To build the average new American house, huge amounts of resources are used: ten thousand board feet of framing lumber, thirteen thousand square feet of gypsum wall board, plywood sheathing and exterior siding; fifty cubic yards of concrete; four hundred linear feet of copper and plastic pipe; fifty gallons of paint; and three hundred pounds of nails.[5] All those resources are used to house just a few people.

What do we leave behind after gobbling up all these resources? Consider products like household cleaners, insecticides, paint thinners, dioxins used to produce paper, batteries containing acid and lead, plastics and oil, to name a few. A certain amount of this refuse is dumped in landfills and ends up leaching into underground aquifers near streams and rivers, endangering wildlife, the human food chain, and occasionally creating a hazardous waste site. In addition, the Environmental Protection Agency regulations do not regulate more than half of the chemicals dumped in our waterways.[6] So clearly, when the "monster" consumes natural resources, he always leaves "presents" behind.

One of the main problems right now is a great lack of awareness about conserving the Earth's resources in our own homes, particularly in home decorating and construction. According to David Morris of the

Institute for Local Self-Reliance in Minneapolis, a whopping 40% of the nation's raw materials are used in creating our homes! [7] It is also estimated that American industry produces seven times more goods in 1990 than it did in 1960. [8] It seems that every year, Americans consume more and more resources for everything, including home improvement.

But not all is lost. We can curb our home environment's appetite by using less, making things more efficient, and turning some of this garbage into treasures we can use again. In the decorating world, we call this using reusable and recycled instead of virgin; repairing and sharing instead of disposing and replacing; creating durability instead of obsolescence and using safe and biodegradable products instead of toxic ones. [9] Examples of such home products are carpeting made from recycled plastic bottles, hardwood flooring made from salvaged wood, and bedspreads and towels created from vintage fabrics or organic cotton. Other examples are hardwood furniture made from certified forest lumber, appliances that are water and energy efficient, and paint and household products that are low in toxins and are biodegradable. By reading this book, you will learn how easy it is to obtain many of these Earth-friendly products while creating a comfortable and stylish home.

To some, eco-friendly interior design may conjure up wild and unruly images of trees growing in the middle of a living room, and people sitting around cross-legged in beanbag chairs in a room painted in dull shades of brown and green. This couldn't be further from the truth. Eco-friendly interior design and home improvement simply means using things that are renewable, recyclable, biodegradable or low in toxins. Remember that when you are designing your home with Earthwise products, you are doing two things: You are providing your home with a greater level of comfort and elegance, and you are helping to keep a harmonious balance in the environment by using sustainable products.

Here is a list of questions to ask when shopping for eco-friendly home products.

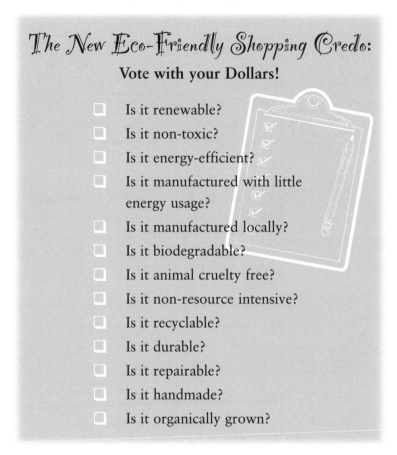

The New Eco-Friendly Shopping Credo:
Vote with your Dollars!

- ☐ Is it renewable?
- ☐ Is it non-toxic?
- ☐ Is it energy-efficient?
- ☐ Is it manufactured with little energy usage?
- ☐ Is it manufactured locally?
- ☐ Is it biodegradable?
- ☐ Is it animal cruelty free?
- ☐ Is it non-resource intensive?
- ☐ Is it recyclable?
- ☐ Is it durable?
- ☐ Is it repairable?
- ☐ Is it handmade?
- ☐ Is it organically grown?

By using eco-friendly products, you can make home improvements more interesting and gratifying. You will also be creating a home of natural and simple elegance that will provide endless hours of joy and rejuvenation; a place where you can breathe and feel in harmony with nature, where you have lessened your impact on the Earth's resources. Above all, you will have created a home that is beautiful, healthy and comfortable. With this approach, your home can become a showcase for your friends and family to admire and emulate.

You can be a pioneer. The whole idea of this book is to turn your home, room by room or project by project, into an eco-friendly jewel you can be proud of! By reading this book, you will discover that eco-friendly decorating is both simple and within reach; something that can fit easily into your yearly budget goals using readily available products. While some think that environmentally friendly products are expensive and only for an elite few, this need not be so. Granted, many Earth-friendly products may cause a little sticker shock. But in the end, most eco-friendly products actually help you save money, in many cases, quite a bit of money. So let those old notions evaporate and let's decorate away!

One way this book will help you keep within your budget is by providing you with estimated product prices and charts to help you prioritize projects, year by year, according to your time and money. These charts will be handy references to refresh your memory about project priorities and the money allocated to each one. Keep this book in your car glove compartment so that when you go shopping it will be there as a reminder and checklist.

And, while you are creating your own personal haven, this book will help you discover and eliminate sources of indoor smog and toxins by helping you avoid products associated with them. According to the Environmental Protection Agency (EPA), indoor pollution generated by furnishings and home improvement products is a much larger threat to people than outdoor pollution, averaging one to two hundred times worse. Yet few people take any real action to eliminate it from their homes. If all the noxious vapors inside a home came in the form of bright purple smog, causing us to gag, more people might be inspired to do something about them. However insidious, most forms of indoor pollution are invisible to the naked eye. They have the net effect of slowly and quietly robbing people of their energy and vitality, resulting in a wide range of physical ailments that are often attributed to anything other than their true source—indoor pollution and toxins. Homes that seem to be afflicted with numerous toxic sources have what is called "sick-building" syndrome.

Have you ever lived or worked in a place, perhaps one that was freshly painted or had new carpeting and furniture in it, where you felt continuously tired, or maybe even had low-grade headaches or coughing? Did you wonder what was wrong with you? Maybe, you thought, you hadn't been eating properly, or were coming down with the flu. Maybe you felt you just needed more sleep. Did you ever consider that the source of your malaise might be coming from household products such as paint, carpeting and cleaning solutions?

When I visit design show rooms and retail stores, I hear constant complaints from the sales people in various departments about feeling sick and having severe allergies. It's funny how easily you can get allergy-tested for pollen, animal dander and molds. But, when it comes to toxins coming from products like vinyl, formaldehyde-based furniture, cleaning products, paints, varnishes and pesticides, few tests exist. Is something wrong with this picture? Although the EPA is interested in testing some products to make sure they are not carcinogenic, the public is largely on their own when it comes to products causing other ailments. This book will help you spot these hidden toxic monsters before they spot you, and will guide you while shopping for furnishings and products that are non-toxic and healthy.

Room by room, this book will guide you in creating a master plan for your living space—making every room as eco-friendly, beautiful and comfortable as possible. Together, we will create the home of your dreams.

This manual is organized one room at a time. This is the best way to focus your energies in order to avoid the possibility of costly decorating mistakes and lack of design harmony. A comprehensive plan for each room will help you keep within your budget and design priorities. Remember, you don't need to make all the changes suggested in every chapter. Just knowing what's possible will help you make the changes at your own pace.

❀ ❀ ❀

Chapter 1

GETTING STARTED:
PLANNING, DESIGNING AND
PAINTING YOUR ROOM

*If you don't have a road map,
you will never know where you are going.*

How to Select a Decorating Style or Theme

As you prepare for each room, keep in mind a design theme and an estimated budget. I recommend that you read the chapter about the room you will be working on first, so you have a clearer idea of how your envisioned items are interrelated and how much they will cost, so you can construct a realistic plan and budget. Even though most of us want to incorporate cherished, existing pieces into the design plan, remember to think about them in terms of the whole room, rather than as isolated pieces.

How do you come up with the perfect design theme or style? This is one of the most enjoyable parts of decorating—inventing your dream idea. Once you have selected a starting room, say for instance the bedroom, the next step is to choose a theme and colors. This will give you a direction and a vision.

There are many ways to develop a theme. Perhaps you saw a picture of a room in a decorating magazine that simply took your breath away, or a room that represented the way you feel about you and your life. Maybe you are a nature lover and saw a room that made you feel like you were in an ancient redwood forest full of misty green ferns. The room had relaxing, dark, mossy-green and brown colors, classical animal drawings on the walls, beautiful antiques and an old patina-stained leather chair. Perhaps there is someone whose home you admire. Whenever you visit, you feel invigorated and uplifted by the jazzy, bright red and white contemporary décor and you would like to feel that way in your own home.

There are many ways to create your own design theme. Just look around. Your heart will know when you see something you love. Have some scissors handy so you can cut pictures out of a home magazine to file. Keep a small camera in your glove compartment or purse. Whenever you see something you like, whether it is a design theme or any other thing for your house, take a picture. Once you decide on a theme, you can refer to this picture again and again. I suggest that you take a picture of every room in your home that you would like to decorate. Put these photos in an envelope and keep them in your glove compartment. That way, if you are in a store and you happen to see something you love, you can refer to that photo to have a better sense of whether if it is the right color, style, and size for the room.

While you are out searching for ideas, you may find that you gravitate towards the rich, warm and elegant look of Mediterranean-style furniture and design. Or maybe you've fallen in love with the earthy colors and natural appeal of Arts and Crafts design. You can even mix styles to create your own eclectic look, although this may be a little more difficult than sticking to one theme. These are the types of things you should think about while creating a room theme. Also, keep in mind existing architectural elements, so that your vision is in keeping with the stylistic framework of your house. You also want to consider existing furnishings and carpeting when selecting new colors, styles and fabrics. Even though you are searching for a new look, there will probably be many things you will want to keep for the sake of memories and to save money and resources.

When designing your room, keep in mind its various uses and functions. For instance, if it is a living room, do you need a place for a TV and stereo? Perhaps you have to make space for an entertainment armoire. Do you entertain a lot? Then you will need a comfortable seating arrangement that is good for conversation. Will there be kids playing in the room? If so, then you probably won't want to use delicate fabrics, breakable accessories or furniture with hazardous sharp edges. While creating a beautiful space, you always want to keep function in mind.

A furniture floor plan, or a simple sketch on paper, will show you where all the furniture and design items should be placed, and how many and what types are needed. (To learn how to construct a furniture floor plan, turn to page 113 in the Living Room Chapter). A furniture floor plan will help you select the most appropriate, correctly sized and functional pieces of furniture and design elements, ensuring your room is spatially balanced and will accommodate traffic through and within the room. Without a furniture floor plan, you might find that, after spending lots of time and money decorating, the room still does-n't look or feel quite right. The room might feel lopsided or unbalanced, with one side having  massive vertical furniture and the other side containing smaller, more diminutive, horizontal furniture. The furniture must also be in proportion and scale to the room size. For instance, you don't want to put dollhouse size furniture in an enormous room; or massive furniture designed for a large home in a small room. Another common problem is cluttering a room with furniture that obstructs movement, or makes you feel claustrophobic. A room should flow.

I remember taking a trip to the coast one weekend, and looking around for the best hotel. The place where I thought I was going to stay looked from the outside like a lovely bed and breakfast, with a unique theme. Unfortunately, the place did not live up to my expectations. The lobby reading/entertainment room, where I planned to spend a great deal of time, looked like a warehouse of chairs. I am sure they put chairs there to accommodate large numbers of people, but I just felt like I was swimming in a sea of chairs and coffee tables - not my idea of comfort at all. This room could have benefited greatly from a furniture floor plan. Just a little of bit planning and rearranging can go a long way!

Now that you have a direction for your room, you can begin selecting your furniture and other design products. This book can help you navigate through the many design products, separating the eco-friendly ones from the not so eco-friendly. The combination of a well-planned room and environmentally friendly materials will enhance the sense of unity and harmony in your home.

Choosing a Color Scheme

"The purest and most thoughtful minds are those that love color the most."

—John Ruskin

We all love color, and most peoples' favorite color reflects who they are, even if it is black or white. Colors represent our emotions and attitudes about life. Painting a room is a rare opportunity to luxuriate in your favorite colors and to express who you really are.

What Your Favorite Colors Say About You.

Red-*passionate and powerful*
Blue-*loyal and serene*
White-*pure and clean*
Yellow-*joyful and energetic*
Green-*tranquil and relaxed*
Orange-*extroverted and exuberant*
Purple-*sensual and magical*
Pink-*cheerful and sociable*
Black-*bold and successful*

Choosing a color scheme for your room - Let the fun begin!

Many people have a love/hate relationship with color. They can't wait to spread luscious colors all over their walls and rooms but are afraid of making mistakes, either by making a room look like it was designed by Coco the Clown - one big colorful mess, or by making it look like a bland blend of "nothing" neutrals like a postal mail room. So how do you make that leap and choose the right colors?

First, when selecting room colors, don't just look for the most attractive colors. Remember you are also choosing colors for how they will effect a room. Will they, for instance, make the room look larger or smaller? Do you want the room to have a serene relaxing feel, or do you want people to feel exhilarated and excited the moment they walk in?

Other questions you want to ask yourself are, can you envision and embrace this color selection throughout your home? What other colors would you like to see with your main choice? If you can answer some of these questions, you will find that choosing the right colors is easier than you think.

One of the first things you may want to consider when choosing a room color scheme is whether you want the room to look larger or smaller. If you want it to appear smaller and more intimate, you may want to select a cool color like blue or green, or any darker color. If you want to make a very small room appear larger, warm colors like red, yellow and orange, or any pale color, are probably your best bets. Lighting can also have an effect on the apparent size of the room. Bright light makes a room seem larger, while dimmer light makes it seem smaller.

Another thing to consider when selecting room colors is what sort of impact they will have on peoples' emotions. If you want people to feel joyful and excited, then go for warmer colors like red, yellow and orange. If you envision people feeling relaxed and peaceful in your room, then you might want to consider cool colors like blues and greens.

When choosing a color group for a room, it is good to pick out at least three or more different colors. The first will be the dominant or leading color, the next will be the second most common color and the third will be the accent, or the least common color, used for a splash of detail.

The rough proportions between these colors should be about 60:30:10, and should be distributed at three different levels in the room: at floor level, at mid or furniture level, and above eye level on the walls, windows or ceilings. Along with these colors, it is also good to add neutrals like beige, white, gray or black to your scheme to let the eye rest and to add visual interest and harmony.

Once you have selected your color group, decide if this is something you want to use in just one room or throughout your home. This decision is determined by the size of your home. If you have a large home, there is more space to try different color themes in different rooms, but this works best if there is harmony at the meeting points of the walls and floors of each room and if the colors, textures and patterns look well coordinated and balanced in corridors and when room doors are open.

If you have a smaller home, it is best to stick with the same color group to achieve a harmonious balance throughout. For instance, if the colors yellow, green and beige are your love, you might have one room with yellow walls, beige carpeting, and beige and green furniture; while in another room, you can have a variation with dark hard wood floors, yellow and beige upholstery, and beige and green patterned window treatments.

What if you want to incorporate more than three colors? How many colors can you actually have in a room? Three colors is a good, workable number for any room's large decorative areas like floors, upholstery and window treatments. However, if you want to use additional colors, you can incorporate them as accents in accessories or other small decorative details like cushions and trims. You can be as creative as you wish; these basic guidelines will give you the structure and direction you need.

How to Choose Paint Colors

A good paint job is one of the most important decorating projects, since it covers such a huge amount of surface space and defines a room's color palette. It is often best to wait until you have chosen your design theme and color scheme before you spend hours applying paint. Many of us are tempted to "initiate" a room and make it our own by painting it as soon as we move in. Often, we realize later that the color doesn't go with the furniture that ends up in the room and have to repaint, resulting in a waste of time, money and materials.

One way of choosing your colors is to select one or more other design items on which to base a new theme, mood or direction. These items can be anything from a new comforter, to a painting, window treatment, an area rug or even a picture from a home magazine. For example, if your mind is set on creating a country-style room in cool peaceful colors, you might want to find a picture that has these elements. An example might be a picture of an Italian country farm in spring, containing yellows, greens and blues, which are the colors for the rest of the room. This is the focal piece that will make everything happen.

There are literally hundreds of paint colors to choose from so it is much easier to paint after you find certain design products rather than vice versa. For instance, if you discover a blue and white floral comforter that is the most beautiful thing you ever laid eyes on, what are you going to do if you have already painted the room peach? A match? You bet not! The moral of this story is to think before you paint. (If you want to go the safe route though, you can always choose white, which goes with almost anything.)

What to do at the Paint Store

One way to choose your paint color is to take a photo or some fabric from the design item you have selected like a painting, comforter, window treatment, area rug etc., and bring it to the paint shop. Try to find a store that can give you plenty of personal attention and that uses a computerized paint coloring system. If the store mixes paint colors by hand, there is a good chance your paint color will look different than what was on the swatch, especially if the person mixing the paint is not experienced or is in a rush. For instance, you may have selected a salmon color that actually turns out brownish-beige on the wall—not at all what you wanted!

After finding the right paint store, hold up the fabric or photo to all the paint swatches you like at the store and select about six or eight. Put them away for a few minutes so you can look at them again from a fresh perspective. Then, from among those colors, buy three sample paint quarts or paint pockets of the color grouping you like best. Bring them home and try them out on either white poster board, Sheetrock,® a white wall or an old piece of plywood coated with white primer. If you are using board, make sure that you hold up this painted board in the exact room you will be painting. Before deciding on the color, make sure the paint is completely dry and that you have observed the colors at different times of the day under different lighting conditions. Daylight shadows, contrasting room colors and the colors of carpeting or cabinetry can alter the color of the paint dramatically. (Remember, sometimes the swatch color is not necessarily the color that comes out on your wall). You may have to try a few different samples to get it right.

Most brands of paint come in at least four levels of sheen. For both visual and practical reasons, selecting the right sheen is very important. Gloss paints offer the highest light-reflectivity. Following gloss in declining order of sheen are semi-gloss, satin, eggshell and flat paints. The right sheen can extend the life of a paint job. Typically, higher sheen levels are usually more durable, while lower sheen levels have greater capabilities for hiding flaws and blemishes. So, you might want to use a semi-gloss for a child's room for its stain resistance and washability, but use a flatter paint for masking drywall or in an elegant living room for its chic texture.

If you are painting the walls of a living room, dining room or bedroom, from the colors you have chosen, try using one that's in the middle of the color range on your sample swatch in flat paint or eggshell. For the woodwork or trim, it is often a good idea to choose the lightest color in either eggshell or semi-gloss paint. For ceilings less than nine feet tall, select a paint color two shades lighter on the swatch than the wall paint in flat paint. Or if it is higher than nine feet, paint it one shade darker than the wall paint. Only after experimenting, and finding the right shades, will it be time to buy the paint quarts or gallons.

Remember to save your chosen paint swatches by putting them in an envelope with all your other room colors. These can be used to make a sample/color board to refer to when selecting window treatments, accessories, upholstery etc. (Refer to page 108 for constructing a sample/color board.) Save left over paint for future touch-ups.

Preparing the Surface for Painting

Before you paint, look at the wall surfaces carefully under bright light. Scrape any loose paint and fill any cracks or dings with a spackling compound. Lightly sand any rough spots or glossy surfaces with 220-grit sandpaper.

Now give your walls a good scrub-down with low-toxic TSP cleaner (Trisodium phosphate). This will take off most of the dirt and grime. Make sure you wash off the TSP before applying primer. Follow the cleaning with a first coat of white primer.

How to Paint Over Wallpaper

If you want to paint over wallpaper, scrape off the peeling areas, and then apply a skim coat of thinned joint compound. Before painting, sand this area and seal with a stain-blocking primer, which will prevent the wallpaper colors from showing through the primer.

Painting Supply List

Bring this list with you when buying paint.

1) Primer
2) Paint
3) Drop cloth-To protect the furniture and floors from paint.
4) TSP (Trisodium phosphate)-To clean walls before putting on primer.
5) Bucket-Fill with water and clean dirty brushes in it.
6) Painter's tape

7) 2" durable angular brush for windows and trim
8) 1"-4" brushes for walls and doors (4" for largest areas and 2.5" for trim)
9) Step ladder
10) Old cloth rags
11) Roller
12) Paint roller tray
13) Screw driver for opening paint can
14) Paint mixing stick
15) Trash can lined with plastic bag
16) Scissors or utility knife
17) Cotton gloves
18) Paint scraper
19) Surfacing compound
20) Caulk and caulk gun
21) Putty knife
22) 220-grit sandpaper
23) A patient mind set!
24) Music!

Toxic Precautions

When painting, try to paint in good weather so you can open windows to ventilate the room. Pregnant women should not paint. If you suspect there may be any lead in the paint you are scraping off the walls, make sure you call in a lead paint abatement professional for sanding or scraping. (Refer to p. 24 for more details.)

Low-VOC Paint - Paint that is odorless, nontoxic and less harmful to the environment

Cost: Low-VOC paint-$27.00 p/gal
High Quality Conventional Latex Paint-$25.00 p/gal

Fortunately, more and more paint stores carry low-VOC (volatile organic compound) paints and stains, that off-gas very little noxious fumes and do less harm to the environment, for only a dollar or two extra per gallon. Although you may not find this paint by a label that says low-VOC in big writing, you can find this water-based paint in many stores labeled as "low-odor," "low-VOC," "low-solvent" or "safe." Make sure to ask which paints have lower VOC values, or lower solvent levels; information easily found in the store's paint literature. You can purchase low-VOC paints from retailers like Sherwin-Williams, Miller Paints, Benjamin Moore Paints and Rodda Paints, as well as from eco-friendly specialty catalogues and retailers. You may not always be able to find all the rich, bold and intense colored hues in low-VOC paint, but you are likely to find all your softer, paler colors and primers in low-VOC paint. One major problem with most low-VOC paints is that it takes more coats to get complete coverage compared to conventional paints. The best place to get high quality low-VOC paints is at environmental building supply stores and catalogs.

It is estimated that a full nine percent of ground-level ozone pollution is attributed to toxic solvents in building paint![10] In the United States alone, we use more than a billion gallons of paint each year. Traditional, solvent-based interior paints can be toxic as they may emit off-gases (VOCs) such as vinyl chloride, benzene, toluene and acetone, which can cause an array of health problems including dizziness, allergic reactions and respiratory ailments.

Although the paint industry is still poorly regulated, some states have established health and environmental standards and regulations that require major public building projects such as health care facilities, schools and office buildings to use low-toxic and low-VOC water-based products for interior paint jobs. Unfortunately, there have been far fewer requirements for the residential sector.[11] Sherwin Williams, Benjamin Moore, Rodda Paint and Miller, are examples of major manufacturers who are taking the lead in offering low-toxic paints for public use. They also offer coordinating paint products like water-based acrylic latex primers and enamels, all of which are low-VOC and odor-free.

When you have finished painting, if you have leftover paint that you don't need to save for touch-ups, some of the larger home retail stores will take back paint originally purchased from them, and resell it for a dollar or two as "whoops" paint -as long as the paint can isn't too messy. Some municipal communities also have programs that will accept your leftover paint, and use it or resell it to the general population at a heavily discounted price. Whatever you do, don't throw unused wet paint in the garbage or flush it down the drain. If you can't bring it to a toxic dump facility, dry it out. There are two ways you can do this: One is to paint a piece of scrap cardboard with the unused water-based paint and let it dry before throwing it away. The other is to buy a packet of relatively expensive waste paint hardener, which you add to a can of unused paint so that it can harden and dry before you throw the paint away. When paint is dry it is no longer environmentally harmful since paint mainly off-gases when wet.

What do I do with the left over paint ?

Recycled Paint

> Price: Recycled Paint-$12.00 per gallon
>
> Price: Conventional paint-$15.00-$35.00 per gallon

Another good paint value is recycled latex paint made from collected and re-blended surplus latex paint. As a post-consumer product, it cuts down on waste and offers a good economic value. It is usually very inexpensive, comes in a variety of colors and is very durable and easy to apply since it often combines several types of paint.

Milk Paint
For Brighter Hues and a "Hand Crafted" Look

If you are in pursuit of a unique look, and wish to depart from the softer colors traditional for the bedroom and bathroom, you have an eco-friendly painting option in the more intense, Earth toned hues of milk paints. These paints have milk as their natural and primary base. They tend to create a handcrafted look and are inclined to be a little more challenging than regular paints in terms of preparation and application. But, if you have an adventurous spirit, go for it and you may find yourself so enthusiastic about milk paint that you'll want to use them again and again. One exciting thing about milk paints is that, by in using them, you are recreating a little bit of history. Paints like these are made from silica, clays and natural waxes, and were used in ancient Greece, Mexico and Egypt.

Lead in Paint

If you live in a house built before 1980, there is a chance that it was painted with lead-based paint. About 40 percent of homes in the U.S. still contain lead paint layers. Lead paint was banned in the U.S. in 1978, but 25 percent of these still pose a significant health hazard.[12]

Signs of lead toxicity are weakness, loss of appetite, vomiting, and anemia. High lead levels can also damage the central nervous system and are linked to learning disabilities, high blood pressure, and kidney damage.

Lead-based paint is the primary source of lead poisoning in children who may eat or chew on paint chips or other surfaces that contain lead, or even more significantly, come into contact with lead dust while playing on the floor.

By the age of six, up to 2 percent of the nation's children have ingested enough lead to harm their bodies and brain.[13]

Lead poisoning can also occur when lead-containing dust is inhaled during remodeling.

The level of lead toxicity will depend primarily on what year the lead paint was made. Before 1950, paint, varnishes and other coatings commonly used contained lead levels of up to 50 percent. After 1950, the use of lead-based paint declined, along with the lead content of the paint, but lead-based paint continued to be sold on the market until the mid-1970's.

The good news is that if you do discover lead-based paint in your home, it is not necessarily an immediate health threat unless it is inhaled or swallowed. Home lead test kits are a good start, but they are not always completely accurate. The best way to determine whether your house contains hazardous levels of lead is to have it evaluated by a lead inspection professional who can recommend the safest and most cost-effective way to remove the lead. Try to avoid having a lead "removal" professional inspect your home because of the possible conflict of interest. Do not try to remove lead paint by yourself. For a list of contacts in your area or for more information call The National Lead Information Center at 1-800-424-Lead.

Your community's local health department or agency can test paint, dust, water or soil samples for you, or refer you to a qualified professional. Two good sources for finding information and help about lead testing and removal are the EPA's web sites: www.epa.gov/opptintr/lead/leadpdfe.pdf and www.epa.gov/lead/rrpamph.pdf. The latter will refer you to state agencies that can assist you in finding an authorized lead abatement specialist in your area, as well as possible financial assistance. If you have children under six and suspect your home contains lead, ask your pediatrician to conduct the recommended tests, or contact the local health department to find where to have your children tested for lead.

❀ ❀ ❀

Chapter 2

THE BATHROOM

MAKE YOUR BATHROOM CLEAN AND GREEN (BUT NOT MOLDY!)

Create a Budget for Your Room

ITEM	Approximate Cost
Cost Estimates-	
Wallpaper	$10-$120 per roll
Paint	$15-$40 per gallon
Window Treatments	$75-$200+per average size window
Tile	$4.00+/sq. ft. uninstalled
Vinyl Flooring	$1.00-$6.00+/sq. ft. uninstalled
Bamboo Flooring	$7.00-$10.00+/sq. ft. uninstalled
Wood Flooring	$4.00-$10.00+/sq. ft. uninstalled
Cork Flooring	$7.00-$10.00+/sq. ft. uninstalled
Stone	$3.00-$30.00+/sq. ft. uninstalled
Concrete	$5.00-$20.00+/sq. yd. installed
Sconce Lights	$40-$1,000+
Ceiling Light	$40-$1,000+
Over-the-Mirror Lights	$50-$1,000+

Do you want to give your bathroom a whole new look? All it may need is a simple sprucing up by changing the paint color, replacing the shower curtain or installing new light fixtures. You can take it even further by adding more shelves, cabinets and accessories. If your bathroom is terribly unattractive or falling apart, you might need a complete remodel. This would involve installing new flooring, cabinets and countertops.

This chapter will describe Earthwise options for bathroom design and provide information about environmental pitfalls like radon, lead in the water, and water conservation. Let your new bathroom become a sanctuary for cleansing and relaxation, not a place that drains your energy and pocketbook!

Decorating A Bathroom

Estimated Budget-
A Simple Spruce Up: $200-$1,000+
A Complete Remodeling Job: $7,000-$40,000+

A Simple Bathroom Makeover

If you decide on a quick bathroom makeover, follow these simple guidelines for a fresh new look. First, decide how your choice of colors, style, furnishings, lighting and accessories can help achieve your vision. For those with smaller bathrooms, this can be particularly challenging since you have fewer design options to work with.

A good place to start is selecting your color palette. One easy way of doing this is to choose a shower curtain and work your way from there. These come in a vast array of colors, patterns and styles. Choose a shower curtain that has one or more of the colors you want to use for the rest of the room. Remember that the colors and design of the shower curtain will dominate and set the tone for the entire room. Also, keep in mind what style you would like for your bathroom. Would you prefer a sleek contemporary look, a traditional look or maybe something warm and cozy?

Although more limited in color and design than vinyl or cotton shower curtains, an Earthwise choice are those made from hemp or organic cotton. Conventional cotton curtains are much less Earthwise, since conventional cotton is grown with excessive pesticides and fertilizers. Still, conventional cotton fabric is a better choice than PVC or vinyl curtains, which off-gas harmful chemicals and are manufactured in an environmentally unfriendly way.

Once you have selected your shower curtain, the walls come next. Select the wall color with the color, pattern and style of the shower curtain in mind. Among the simpler options are to paint, wallpaper or do a combination of the two. If you are going to paint your bathroom, use semi-gloss paint, which is very washable and great for high moisture areas. Pale pastel colors usually work best for bathroom walls.

Wallpaper

The Chinese invented wallpaper in 200 B.C.

Wallpaper can be a tempting substitute for paint, but you will want to use it sparingly as a border or such, and to choose the right type of paper. Many waterproof types of wallpaper are made of vinyl, which off-gases harmful vapors. Vinyl wallpaper is also not breathable, trapping moisture that creates mold and mildew problems. This can be an issue in the bathroom and kitchen where excessive moisture is present. Wallpaper can be expensive and difficult to remove, and if removed improperly, can result in the need for resurfacing the walls underneath.

If you are thinking about removing wallpaper, you may be happy to learn that you can usually just paint over it. Before doing this, test it to make sure the paper is still securely in place, and then seal it with a stain blocking primer to prevent the colors from bleeding through when painting over it. To remove wallpaper, use hot water or steam with a bit of baking soda added to it.

Fortunately, there are a few alternatives to vinyl wallpaper on the market, but they are better suited for rooms without a high moisture content. One type of eco-friendly wallpaper is grass cloth, which is made from jute, rush or arrowroot. Prices start at $30.00 per roll and go up to $100.00. Other wallpaper options are maps, gift-wrap and even newspaper, which make funky, one-of-a kind wall coverings. If you do decide to use wallpaper, try buying organic glue because most wallpaper pastes have chemical adhesives and fungicides that can irritate the skin.

Bathroom Lighting
Light Up Your Beauty, Not Your Imperfections!

Good morning! You wake up and crawl out of bed, and if you are like most people, one of the first things you do is hobble to the bathroom and take a quick peek in the mirror just to make sure you are still alive. What do you want to see-the sleeping beauty or the morning ogre? That is why it is so important to have bathroom lights that enhance you (not your imperfections), and make your bathroom tasks a lot easier.

Ideally, a bathroom should have several sources of light. One should be either a hanging or recessed overhead light with an Earthwise CFL (compact fluorescent bulb). For a well-lit effect, choose a bulb with a high wattage that casts a broad spectrum of light.

For task lighting, or balanced lighting that will enhance your face and not cast harsh shadows, place lights on both sides of the mirror, ideally between 28"-42" apart. If space doesn't permit, the next best choice is to install a multi-bulb fixture directly above the mirror.

If you feel the bathroom still needs more light, consider adding wall sconces that will direct light gently upwards. Another good idea is to add a skylight that will radiate natural light during the day, saving money on your electric bill.

Bathroom Furniture and Cabinets

For bathroom furniture and cabinets, consider vintage pieces, glass, metal or bamboo shelves, as well as straw board, wheat board, bamboo or certified wood cabinets.

If you have an antique or vintage look in mind, try combing through antique stores and garage/estate sales. Bamboo furniture and shelves can give your bathroom a sleek, exotic or Asian look, while at the same time allowing you to support an alternative wood industry.

If you decide on taking the full remodeling plunge, here are some ideas about what to do with your cabinets, countertops and floors.

Cabinets - Make the Right Choice for You and the Earth

The best way to choose bathroom cabinets, countertops and flooring is to visit different bathroom showrooms to see and feel what's available. Ask questions about storage needs, detailing, cost, care and maintenance.

When looking for bathroom cabinets, consider your storage needs. Do you need a medicine cabinet, or other cabinets for your bathroom supplies and equipment? As a rule of thumb, allow one square foot of storage for every person using the washbasin.

Cabinets made from certified forest wood, available from sources like Neil Kelly, come from well-managed, ecologically sound forests. Furthermore, when you get your furniture from a company that uses straw board, wheat board or FSC certified wood, you can usually count on low or non-toxic paints, finishes and oils being used for finishing.

For more information on Earthwise cabinets, turn to page 45 in the kitchen chapter.

Bathroom Countertops And Floors
Beautiful Earthwise Surfaces

Bathroom Countertops–
Tile, Stone, Concrete, and Wood

Cost Estimates
Ceramic Tile - $4.00+/sq. ft. uninstalled
Slate - $3.50-$22.00/sq. ft. uninstalled
Granite - $5.00-$31.00/sq. ft. uninstalled
Marble - $5.00-$27.00/sq. ft. uninstalled
Travertine - $5.00-$15.00/sq. ft. uninstalled
Concrete - Cost is similar to granite
Wood - $4.00-$10.00/sq.ft. uninstalled
Tile Installation - $5.00-$10.00/sq. ft.
Stone Installation - $8.00-$15.00/sq.ft.

Simple, elegant, tough and non-polluting, ceramic tiles, stone and concrete work well for countertop surfaces. If possible, buy local materials instead of those shipped across the country or worse yet, from overseas, which consumes large quantities of precious energy. If possible, try to save money and resources by buying salvaged samples or in the case of tile, tile made from recycled materials like glass windshields or bottles.

Tiles - Tile Your Way to Uniqueness

Available in hundreds, if not thousands, of different colors and designs, tiles are one way of making your bathroom unique. However, tiles can be pricey and expensive to install, especially the hand-designed ones which many people consider works of art. Tiles can also chip or scratch during normal bathroom use. Even though tiles can be quite durable, the grout has a tendency to stain. A good grout sealer will seal the surface that helps prevent staining. **For more information on tiles refer to p. 35.**

Gorgeous Stone Surfaces

Granite - Tough and Elegant

Popular, plentiful and extremely tough, granite is a good kitchen and bathroom countertop and flooring choice since it is scratch, stain and heat resistant, and is usually mined locally within the United States. Granite does, however, need to be sealed at least once a year to prevent staining since it is porous. Granite comes in colors like pink, white, red, beige and black.

Marble - For a Touch of History

Considered the most ancient and durable of flooring materials, the commercial definition of marble is any rock that can take a polish. Having been used for centuries in the world's grandest buildings like the Taj Mahal, nothing quite surpasses marble for mystique and elegance. But if you are looking for materials that are Earthwise, economical and practical, marble may not be your best choice, since it sometimes needs to be imported, can be expensive and has a tendency to stain easily if you spill acids like lemon juice or wine on it. Marble also needs to be sealed on a regular basis to prevent staining, and because of this, is best suited for bathroom floors, vanities and entryways.

Slate - Select Slate for a Sleek Look

Slate is ideal for entryways, bathroom floors and vanities, but is not recommended for kitchens since it can chip and stain easily with its porous and uneven surface. Slate comes in an interesting array of colors that range from purple to yellow to red and black, and can be relatively inexpensive. Slate is an elegant, hard and fine-grained stone that often comes from within the United States, thereby eliminating excessive energy use in overseas shipping. If you are buying slate, make sure to get a non-fading variety that will not change color as time goes by. Since slate is one of the most porous flooring stones, it needs special sealants, finishes and cleaning solutions.

Travertine - For a Rough-Hewn Look

Travertine is best suited for bathroom flooring, vanities, showers and vertical surfaces. The product of mineral springs, travertine comes in shades ranging from cream to brown. Because of its rough and open grains, this stone has primarily been used outdoors until fairly recently, when tumbling and sand blasting technologies have made it more suitable for indoors. This product needs periodic sealing.

Concrete Mixture Countertops - Chic and Unique

If you would like to try a beautiful yet non-traditional product, Syndecrete® concrete fly ash counters are worth considering. Made of fly ash and post- consumer scrap materials like metal shavings, crushed glass, scrap wood and plastic chips, this product is made from recycled materials and needs relatively little energy to produce. The only drawbacks to this type of countertop, is that it needs to be sealed and waxed twice a year, and sometimes it can crack.

Bathroom Flooring

In choosing bathroom flooring, tile, stone, linoleum, cork, concrete, bamboo, or certified or salvaged wood are your best Earthwise picks.

Bathroom Flooring

Cost Estimates-
Tile - $4.00-$20.00+/sq. ft. uninstalled
Tile Installation - $5-$10.00/sq.ft.
Vinyl Flooring - $1.00-$6.00/sq. ft. uninstalled
Stone - $3.00-$30.00/sq. ft. uninstalled
Stone Installation - $8.00-$15.00/sq. ft.
True Linoleum - $4.00-$6.00+/sq. ft. uninstalled
Cork - $7.00-$10.00+/sq. ft. uninstalled
Wood - $4.00-$10.00+/sq. ft. uninstalled
Concrete - $5.00-$20.00+/sq. yd. installed

Bamboo $7.00-$10.00+/sq. ft. uninstalled
Granite - $5.00-$27.00+/sq. ft. uninstalled
Slate - $3.50-$22.00+/sq. ft. uninstalled
Marble - $5.00-$27.00+/sq.ft. uninstalled
Travertine - $5.00-$15.00+/sq. ft. uninstalled

For more information on other flooring and countertop materials:

Cork, refer to p. 52	Concrete, refer to p. 34 & 53
Stone, refer to p. 49	Vinyl, refer to p. 53
Wood, refer to p. 98	Linoleum, refer to p. 52
Bamboo, refer to p. 47 & 88	PaperStone™, refer to p. 50
Richlite®, refer to p. 50	Eleek™, refer to p. 51

Bathroom Tiles

If you want your bathroom to be a true "knock out", consider redoing it with tile. Tiles come in a seemingly infinite array of shapes, colors, patterns and themes. If you find the right tile store, you may be swept away by all the possibilities.

Tiles do have a few disadvantages. One disadvantage is that if you don't live in a warm climate or a house that is continuously warm, tiles can be cold on the feet. Some people have overcome this problem through radiant heating, which is warming the floor with electrical heat strips or hot water pipes underneath. Another problem with tile floors is that some can be slippery. When shopping for tile, make sure to get non-skid tiles.

Before you decide to take the plunge and install new bathroom tiles, if you have existing tiles, ask yourself if there is a way to dress up the room without retiling, which means spending more money and using more resources. Can you redecorate simply by repainting and adding a few new towels? Don't get stuck on one idea. Spend time brainstorming about all the possibilities. It's a lot easier to grab a paint brush instead of a jackhammer!

If you decide to buy new tiles, remember that it can be expensive. Bathroom tiles, especially decorative and unusual ones, can be quite costly. But if you are creative and choose lower-priced tiles accented with a few, more expensive ones, you should be able to keep the price down.

The good news about tiles is that they are often quite Earthwise, since they usually come from an abundant resource - clay! Glass tiles made from recycled materials like bottles or car windshields are even more eco-friendly. Also, if possible, try to get locally made tiles instead of tiles made half way around the world. This supports your local tax base and saves energy.

Installing tiles

You may want to consider hiring an experienced tile installer since tiling can be tricky. For a non-toxic bathroom, use a non-toxic grout like C-Cure® and a mortar with a latex additive, which doesn't off-gas much once it's dry. Because grout is porous cement, you may also want to use a non-toxic sealant.

Measuring and purchasing tiles

1) First, determine where you want the tile. In most bathrooms, you'll want to tile up to the 4-foot level above the floor. In a shower, the tiles should reach 6 inches above the showerhead.

2) Decide where you want the field and the trim or accent tiles. Field tiles are the basic tiles that cover most of the surface. Accent or trim tiles are pieces that usually have the most pattern and theme, and are often placed on the edges and corners.

3) To measure, determine the length and width of the tiling area and multiply to come up with your square footage. To find out how many cartons of tile you need, divide the square footage you need covered by the square footage contained in the carton. Add 5 to 10 percent to allow for any mistakes, breakage and future spare tiles.

Bathroom Finishing Touches

Finally, when all the basic design elements are in place, give your bathroom an exciting new look by finding window treatments and accessories that will make your bathroom uniquely yours. Consider installing mildew-resistant honeycomb blinds to keep the room warm, cozy and energy-efficient. You can also add organic cotton towels and bath rugs for a soft, naturally textured look. A candle or two adds a fragrant sense of mystery and allure to the room when soaking in the tub. Finally, if you need more space for storage, add glass or bamboo shelves on the walls and/or above the toilet.

Bathroom Ventilation
Prevent Mold and Noxious Gases from Building Up

It is important to make sure your bathroom is adequately ventilated. This will prevent mold, mildew, peeling paint, and will diminish toxic chemical off-gassing. Before doing anything, make sure to open bathroom windows on a regular basis. Also, consider installing a bathroom fan vented to the outdoors. Choose a quiet model with a CFM (cubic feet per minute) rating of at least 100, which means it exchanges 100 cubic feet of air per minute. It is best to use the fan immediately after taking a shower or bath.

Bathroom Water Conservation
Don't let your water go down the drain!

How can we conserve water, both throughout our homes and in our bathrooms where 75 percent of the water used in American households is consumed?

The average American now consumes 43 million gallons of water in his or her lifetime. [14]

If every person in the world used as much water as an average American, we would exceed the amount of fresh water available in the world.

Indoor Water Conservation
The average person's daily water use

Flushing toilet	30%
Leaky toilets	5%
Shower and Bathing	30%
Clothes Washer	20%
Dishwashing	4%
Faucets	11%

Toilet Water Conservation Tips

The toilet is a very wasteful household appliance, using between 1.6 to 5 gallons of clean tap water per flush, and about 30 percent of the total American household water usage.

If you have an older 3.5 or 5-gallon flush model, start by installing a water displacement device like a one-quart plastic water bottle filled with water in your toilet. The old trick of putting a brick in your toilet tank is not usually the most effective method, since the brick can chip and damage your plumbing parts.

Also, make sure to fix any toilet leak promptly, because a run-away leak can waste up to seventy to one hundred gallons per day. You can tell if a toilet is leaking by putting food coloring in the tank. Let it sit for 30 minutes. If there is a leak, color will appear in the toilet. After the experiment, flush the toilet right away so the food coloring doesn't stain the toilet.

If you are in the market for a new toilet, look for a low-flush model. Fortunately, federal law requires that most new models use only 1.6 gallons per flush; older models used 3.5 to 5 gallons.

Also, consider not flushing every time, especially if you live in an area with limited water supplies.

Faucet Tips

Instead of letting the water run continuously, turn the water on and off as needed when brushing teeth or shaving. This can save up to ten to twenty gallons per use.[15]

If there is any leak, fix it immediately. A leaky faucet can waste nearly 200 gallons of water per month.[16]

Also, consider getting a faucet head aerator. This inexpensive home improvement device blends air into water flow, cutting faucet water consumption by more than half.

Shower/Bath Water Saving Tips

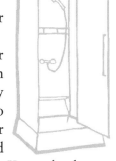

Here are some important ways to limit your usage.

To begin with, it is always better to take a shower than a bath since baths can use up to twice as much water. Also, install a low-flow showerhead, preferably one that removes chlorine so you won't have to breathe or absorb the toxic by-products through your skin. Get into the habit of using "gray water," or used shower/bath water, to water plants or flush the toilet. Keep a bucket or kitchen pot nearby. The soap/shampoo won't hurt the plants, and may actually help fertilize them.

Handy Dandy
Bathroom Water Saving Techniques

1) Install low-flow devices on your shower and sink spigots.
2) Take showers instead of baths. The average shower uses twenty-five gallons while the average bath uses sixty gallons. If you want to take a bath, try taking a shallow bath.
3) Instead of letting the water run continuously, turn the water off and on as needed when brushing teeth or shaving. This can save up to ten to twenty gallons per usage.

Lead Contamination in Drinking Water
Could Your Water have Lead in it?

When household plumbing materials containing lead corrode or wear away, drinking water can become contaminated. These materials include the lead-based solder commonly used by plumbers in joining copper pipe, as well as brass and chrome-plated brass faucets. Lead-based solder was banned in 1986.

The major source of toxic levels of lead in drinking water is the lead solder that connects metal pipes. Watch for signs that indicate the presence of lead in your pipes:

1) You have non-plastic plumbing and fixtures and/or you notice your pipes are all or partly composed of a dull gray metal that can be easily scratched with a key.
2) Your house has copper plumbing installed before 1985, which may contain lead solder.
3) Your home was built before 1930, when the service connectors in your home or neighborhood may have been made of lead. (Call your local water utility office for more information.)

If you do discover a lead problem in your drinking water, you can treat the water with a reverse osmosis, distillation unit, and to some degree, calcite water filters. Another solution is to run the tap water for 15-30 seconds whenever it has been unused for more than six hours. For more information and water testing sources, call the U.S. EPA, Safe Drinking Water Hot Line at 800-426-4791 or contact the web site: www.epa.gov/safewater.

Radon
Another Home Health Hazard

Radon is a naturally occurring radioactive gas that comes from the breakdown of uranium found in soils throughout the U.S. Radon is a colorless, odorless and invisible gas that can go virtually undetected for years.

Although there are still some scientists who believe radon is not a serious threat, the EPA has estimated that radon in the home causes between 5,000 to 20,000 lung cancer deaths each year, the second highest cause of U.S. lung cancer deaths after smoking. It is estimated that as many as one out of every fifteen houses in the U.S. have radon levels above the EPA recommended action level of 4 (pCi/L) for indoor levels of radon. To understand what a "safe" action level is, it is the same as receiving 200 chest x-rays per year.

Radon exists in every state in the U.S., but is much more prevalent in some states than in others, particularly Colorado, Wyoming and Montana. Building materials like certain bricks, cement and aggregate composed of uranium or phosphate mine tailings or stone, and the composition of the soil beneath buildings in high-density radon regions, are all typical sources of radon. Radon enters a home through foundation cracks and other openings in the floors and walls. It is drawn into the home by a vacuum caused when the air pressure inside the home is lower than the pressure in the ground.

Domestic water systems that use wells can also be a source of radon. Radon removal is best accomplished through exposure to air, which allows the radon gas to escape before entering the home. One method of diluting and dispersing the gas is to install a continuous fan to vent under floor spaces and wall cavities.

Fortunately, it is easy to test for radon. If radon is present in hazardous levels, there are many ways to alleviate the problem. Look up the federal EPA website at www.epa.gov/radon for various testing options.

If you have unsafe home radon levels, take these steps to reduce the radon concentration. Open all air vents and windows a few inches when the weather is warm. Also, seal cracks and other openings in the foundation and hire an approved local contractor with radon alleviation experience for further work. Remember, while radon levels could pose a serious health hazard for your family, it is something that is easily rectified. For more information, contact the Radiation Protection Service at (503) 731-4014 ext. 664.

EPA MAP OF RADON ZONES

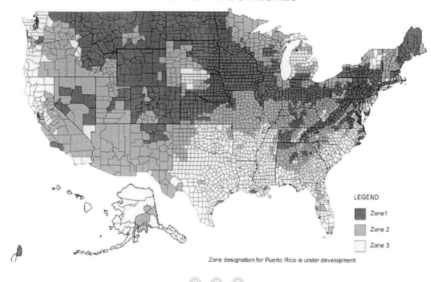

LEGEND

Zone 1
Zone 2
Zone 3

Zone designation for Puerto Rico is under development

Chapter 3

THE KITCHEN

Spicing up Your Earthwise Kitchen

Estimated Budget-
A Simple Spruce-Up-$200-$2,500+
A Complete Remodeling Job-$8,000-$70,000+

Create a Budget for your Room

ITEM	Approximate Cost
Paint	$15- $40 per gallon
Wallpaper	$10- $120 per roll
Hard Window Treatments	$30-$300 per average size window (blinds and shades)
24" Fluorescent Under-the-Cabinet Kitchen Lights	$30.00
24" Halogen Under-the-Cabinet Kitchen Light	$40.00
Sconce Lights	$40-$1,000+
Pendant Light	$75-$2,000+

Vinyl Flooring	$1.00-$6.00+/sq.ft.
True Linoleum	$4.00-$6.00+/sq.ft.
Cork Flooring	$7.00-$10.00+/sq.ft.
Bamboo Flooring	$7.00-$9.00+/sq.ft.
Ceramic Tile	$4.00+/sq.ft.
Granite Countertops	$5.00-$31.00+/sq.ft.
Paperstone™ Countertops	$40-$55+/sq.ft.
Eleek™ Countertops	$95+/sq.ft.
Durat™ Countertops	$85+/sq.ft.
Icestone™ Countertops	$115+/sq.ft.
Tile Installation	$5-$10.00/sq.ft.
Stone Installation	$8.00-$15.00/sq.ft.
Dishwashers	$250-$1,500+
Refrigerators	$400-$1,300+
Washing Machines	$300-$1,500+
Dryers	$200-$850+
Ranges	$300-$1,000+
Microwave Ovens	$40-$600+
Convection Ovens	$179-$1,400+

The kitchen is the pulse of the home. It is where we cook beautiful, nutritious food and have spontaneous "catch-up" conversations with our loved ones. The kitchen is also a place where we can have the greatest home environmental impact by reducing toxic chemicals, and selecting Earthwise cookware, cabinets, countertops, flooring, and appliances. We also want to make sure our kitchen lighting helps us to be more productive and inspires us to cook and eat well.

Kitchen Lighting
Shine the Light on Delicious Delights

Whether you are in your kitchen to cook, for conversation, to make phone calls or simply to relax, you will undoubtedly need a variety of lighting. People should look as good and feel as comfortable in the kitchen as they do in any other room of your house. Often, people make two basic mistakes when designing their kitchen lighting. They install an overhead light that is too bright or not bright enough, or they fail to install enough task lighting. Kitchen lighting should be flexible; a combination of direct task lighting in food preparation and work areas, and soft overhead lighting. For ambient or general illumination, a ceiling or an attractive pendant light, or a series of pendant lights mounted along the centerline of the space, works well, as long as they have the right level of brightness.

For task lighting, consider installing a strong light over the stove and sink, especially if there is not enough constant light. You may also use a hanging pendant light over a kitchen table or eating counter for additional task lighting. Enliven your kitchen countertops with miniature fluorescents installed underneath overhanging cabinets. In addition, you can give your kitchen warmth and depth by mounting compact fluorescent strips over the cabinets. Last, consider installing accent lighting to highlight art pieces. Kitchen lighting should make you feel energized, not drained.

Kitchen Cabinets

The best way to choose kitchen cabinets, countertops and flooring is to visit different kitchen showrooms and see and feel what's available, and ask questions about storage needs, detailing, cost, care and maintenance. Other methods are to surf kitchen Internet websites and read kitchen specialty magazines. Keep all your exciting new finds in an idea file. If you prefer to hire a certified kitchen designer, contact the National Kitchen and Bath Association (NKBA) at www.nkba.org.

Give Your Kitchen an Easy and Inexpensive Makeover

If you are thinking about remodeling your kitchen, you may want to consider refinishing instead of replacing your existing cabinets. If you decide on new cabinets, have a local rebuilding center dismantle the old kitchen for resale to low-income clients. This Earthwise move could also earn you a handsome tax deduction.

Before you decide to get a brand new kitchen, consider giving your existing one an easy face-lift. It's relatively simple to give cabinets a completely new look with fresh paint colors or stains, and with new door faces, knobs or pulls. You can also think about replacing the sink fixtures and kitchen lights if they are in bad shape, refinishing the floors and even installing new countertops. Of course, these additions also consume resources, but they are a good alternative to installing a completely new kitchen.

Recently, a friend decided to install a new kitchen, complete with new light fixtures, new flooring, new countertops and new kitchen cabinets. When it was time for my friend to show off his new creation, he ushered us into his newly designed miniature palace and basked in the glow of enthusiastic reactions. I couldn't help thinking that he could have achieved exactly the same look without spending so much money and wasting all those resources. He could have painted his old pine cabinets white, added some shiny new door pulls, and painted his kitchen walls an exciting new color. To make matters worse, a few years later his new kitchen countertop tiles began to chip. It became clear the new kitchen wasn't nearly as durable as the first.

One option for improving your kitchen cabinets that saves money and wood resources is to install open shelving or a combination of open shelving and cabinets. Why does everything have to be behind closed doors? Another way of making your kitchen especially attractive is storing items like tea bags, sugar, flour or beans in baskets and other decorative containers. This creates an interesting and attractive display.

New Kitchen Cabinet Options

If you decide to replace your cabinets, consider getting new ones made from several alternative sources, such as: straw board, wheat board, certified wood, Plyboo™, Kirei™, or bio-fiber composites; all of which are both Earth-friendly and usually more durable than materials such as particleboard, which can off-gas formaldehyde. Another interesting alternative is to refinish vintage cabinets, which you can purchase from salvage yards, garage/estate sales, classified ads, or even online.

Straw board / Wheat board

By the names, both are made from agricultural waste materials that farmers usually burn in the fields. These products are formaldehyde-free and very durable. The pattern of these bio-composites runs through the entire thickness, allowing for easy repair through simple sanding and refinishing.

Plyboo™ Bamboo

Made of a bamboo veneer over plywood, this product comes in a light and dark version, and can be finished with a water-based urethane. It comes in 4' x 8' sheets in various thicknesses, and in plywood, veneers, and tambour paneling options.

Kirei™

This new product is made from lightweight sorghum. With a front and back veneer, this plywood core product has a very unique and busy appearance. Coming in 3'x 6' sheets and in three different thicknesses, Kirei ™ board is strong, durable, and lightweight.

Low-Toxic Furniture Strippers

Paint strippers are among the most toxic household chemicals around. Fortunately, there are now low toxic, water-based, solvent-free strippers that you can purchase through the same businesses that manufacture low-odor paint. These strippers have less fumes and are much healthier to use than conventional paint strippers.

How to Prevent Formaldehyde Gases from Coming Out of Your Cabinets

If you want to keep your old cabinets but realize they may contain particleboard or plywood that off-gases formaldehyde, there are methods you can use to stop or slow the toxic off-gassing. Keep in mind that the level of formaldehyde off-gassing will diminish over time, particularly after the first five years.

How can you tell if your kitchen or other household cabinets and countertops have formaldehyde-based materials in it? One indicator is that plastic-laminated countertops and cabinets usually have particleboard materials underneath. Also, 90% of all new furniture made in this country is made with formaldehyde-containing pressboard. Open up your kitchen cabinets. Are they made of solid wood? Older models are more likely to be made of formaldehyde-free, solid wood.

If you've determined that your kitchen, bathroom or living room cabinets or countertops are manufactured with formaldehyde, you can prevent off-gassing by sealing the exposed surfaces with three coats of paint or one coat of non-toxic sealer or varnish like shellac. If you do choose to use a shellac product bear in mind that it has a tendency to get darker over time, and can discolor when water gets on a finished surface. In addition, shellac uses alcohol as a base, rather than water or oil, so it is necessary to use denatured alcohol for cleaning.

When sealing cabinets or other furnishings to prevent off-gassing, make sure you seal all exposed surfaces. This includes the bottom face of a laminated counter, inside edges, the surfaces of cupboards and the insides of cabinets.

For more information about formaldehyde, refer to p. 93.

Kitchen Countertops and Floors

Kitchen Countertops - What are Your Earthwise Options?

If you are in the market for new kitchen countertops, there are many gorgeous Earthwise options, including tile and stone, certified wood, recycled paper, glass, and aluminum products, and concrete mixtures. All are attractive, but some tend to stain and are more difficult to clean and maintain. Kitchen countertops, cabinets and floors are the most expensive and resource intensive part of kitchen redesigning, so you may want to consider redecorating before taking the big remodeling plunge with new items.

Tiles - An Opportunity For Creativity

Available in thousands of different designs and colors, tiles are one way to make your kitchen or bathroom truly unique. Tiles, however, can be expensive to install and relatively pricey, especially the hand-designed ones, which many people consider works of art. Tiles can also chip or scratch during normal kitchen use. Even though most tiles are quite durable, the grout has a tendency to absorb stains. A grout sealer will seal the surface so stains are not easily absorbed.

Recycled Glass Tiles

Coming in a wide variety of colors, in either a sanded or clear surface, these tiles make an excellent backsplash. These tiles range in size from from 1 square inch to 6 square inches. Beautiful countertops made from recycled glass and concrete or cement are also available.

Natural Stone

This extremely popular and durable countertop material comes in 8 or 12 square inch tiles, or solid slabs - which have few joint and grout lines. Stone countertops usually cost 30 percent more then tiles. Granite is usually better then marble, being less porous and more heat resistant. For this reason, marble is good for vertical surfaces, such as back splashes.

Granite - Tough and Elegant

Popular, plentiful and extremely tough, granite is a good kitchen and bathroom countertop and flooring choice since it is scratch, stain and heat resistant, and is usually mined locally within the United States. Granite does, however, need to be sealed at least once a year to prevent staining since it is porous. Granite comes in colors like pink, white, red, beige and black.

Wood - A Classic Favorite

If you like the solid earthy look of wood countertops or floors, and don't mind the occasional blemishes, scratches and stains that come with wear and tear, a countertop made of certified or sustainably harvested wood can be a good choice. If you choose wood, make sure you use a nontoxic sealer or polyurethane finish for the general areas, then finish the food preparation areas with salad oil or other plant-based oils such as Ardvose (made by Livos Phytochemistry).

Richlite® - Recycled Paper And Resin Countertop

With a more natural "look" and "feel" than traditional counter-tops, Richlite® is a paper and resin solid surface product with few seams. It comes in six colors with different thicknesses. Unfortunately, it has a tendency to change color when exposed to sunlight.

PaperStone™

This recycled paper product is made up of a water-based resin that is not affected by the sun. If scratched, repair is simple: buff with sand paper and rub down with oil. The oil helps keep it porous. To maintain it's quality it must be treated with oil every six months. This product currently comes in two colors.

Eleek™ - Recycled Aluminum Tile

With a smooth feel, this cast product is made from recycled aluminum, comes in 3, 6, or 12 square inch square tiles and is also available in edging or face tiles. This product is not only expensive, at $95 per square foot, but is also only heat resistant up to 300 degrees; so don't put it near a stove.

Durat™

This recycled plastic and resin product comes in sixty different colors and is imported from Finland. Unlike PaperStone™, it will not show fingerprints, due to its matte finish. With a similar feel and look to Corian™, it is not extremely heat resistant and is expensive.

IceStone™

This unusual product is made from concrete and recycled glass. Coming in more then twenty colors, is both heat resistant and very durable. It also needs to be sealed periodically. Icestone™ is as durable as concrete, but not as porous as marble. This product is expensive.

Engineered Stone - A Stone Substitute

This type of countertop is usually made from quartz combined with resins and pigments. It looks much like granite and is very resistant to stains, heat and scratches. Engineered stone never needs sealing, but it doesn't withstand impact very well.

For information on stone countertops refer to p. 33.
For information on concrete countertops refer to p. 34.

Kitchen Flooring
Cork and Linoleum-Funky, Fashionable, and Replenishable

Cork - A Rich and Earthy Look

Cork was popular in the 1970's and is now making a big comeback. Frank Lloyd Wright used cork in his celebrated "Falling Water" home, built in 1936. Available in a variety of styles, patterns and colors, cork flooring is an eco-friendly home improvement that people easily fall in love with. Made from the bark of the cork tree and harvested every ten years, cork looks great, doesn't rot or grow moldy and is a very effective heat and sound insulator.

Cork comes in pre-finished and unfinished forms. If you have some home improvement experience, you can install it yourself. For some types of cork flooring, the only major piece of equipment required for installation, after the cork is laid and glued, is a hundred pound roller that can be found at equipment rental stores. Cork is available as tiles, which can be glued down with a nontoxic urethane finish or as "floating floors." "Floating click floors" are very easy to install over any existing floor or sub-floor, and have many design options.

Cork currently costs about $7.00 to $13.00+ per square foot, which makes it close in price to bamboo and hardwood flooring, and has a comparable professional installation cost. It is best to shop around as the price and quality of cork can vary greatly. When checking for quality, look for cork tile density. Cork with a higher density and fewer irregularities is more durable and easier to install. Overall, cork is a very durable and tough material that works well for kitchens, living rooms, bathrooms, offices and children's rooms. Keep in mind though, that cork is not a hardwood floor, so it will dent if you put spiked furniture on it.

Like hardwood, cork floors need periodic refinishing. A polyurethane finish is very toxic when applied yet lasts six to eight years. Carnauba wax is nontoxic, but requires yearly reapplication. The choice is yours.

Linoleum Flooring - An old friend revisited
Prices: Vinyl Flooring - $1.00-$6.00+/sq. ft.
      Sheet Linoleum - $3.90-$4.50+/sq. ft.
      Tile Linoleum - $4.00-$6.00+/sq. ft.

True linoleum flooring has become a "hip" alternative to vinyl flooring particularly for kitchens, bathrooms, dens, laundry rooms and commercial spaces. Made of biodegradable, harvestable materials including linseed oil, pine tree resin, wood flour from deciduous trees (combined with fillers such as chalk), linoleum scores high on the eco-friendly hit list. Linoleum flooring is available in sheets, tiles, and easy-to-install click panels and squares. Linoleum comes in an impressive array of colors and patterns. Try to get linoleum that has natural, biodegradable jute or burlap backing, which will not off-gas.

Stay clear of vinyl or PVC flooring. Even though it tends to be less expensive than cork or linoleum, vinyl or PVC requires massive amounts of energy to manufacture, off-gases noxious chemicals and is not biodegradable.

When installing linoleum flooring, it is best to hire a professional flooring contractor with linoleum installation experience, because linoleum has a tendency to crack while being installed and requires professional equipment for heat welding. Linoleum is a good choice for kitchens and bathrooms because it is mildew and mold resistant. Yet, if you are going to install linoleum in the bathroom, make sure that it is sealed around the tub and the perimeter of the room so that water will not go underneath.

Linoleum floors should be refinished twice yearly with an eco-friendly floor finish like *Taski Ombra*. If you want to clean linoleum or cork flooring with a damp mop, make sure not to use excessive amounts of water. Too much water can make the floor buckle. With proper care, your linoleum or cork floor can look beautiful for decades.

Concrete Flooring - Unique and Chic

With a fascinating history that dates back to the Roman Empire, concrete is an ideal flooring material because it is very durable, and is heat, cold and scratch resistant. Concrete floors also offer versatile styling since they can take on any shape or thickness and can be painted, waxed or stained. You can also install radiant heat coils underneath a concrete floor to keep it warm. While you may love the clean modern look, concrete floors are not always easy to install.

Concrete floors need special structural parameters that often include a month of curing to set properly. For this reason, concrete flooring is most appropriate for a new house or as part of a major renovation.

For more information on the following flooring materials:
Tiles-refer to p. 35   Hardwood-refer to p. 87 & 98
Stone-refer to p. 33   Bamboo-refer to p. 88

Plastics and Your Natural Kitchen

We live in a world filled with plastic, but is plastic good for the world? Plastics now litter the shores of the most remote Alaskan islands and the world's tallest snow-capped mountains. Plastic is on the bottom of the ocean, in the bellies of endangered sea turtles and around the necks of sea birds. While we can launch space ships, we have yet to market a widely available and inexpensive biodegradable plastic. In fact, many plastics may outlast the pyramids! When plastics began to be mass-marketed in the 1940's, they were heralded as revolutionary. Who would have thought the revolution would have such unforeseen health and environmental consequences?

Plastics once seemed to be the miracle material of the future. So what's the problem? What has changed and what have we learned? To begin with, plastics are energy hogs. It takes more energy to manufacture plastic than just about any other home or building material including aluminum or even steel. Plastic is made from a nonrenewable resource-petroleum, and is rarely biodegradable. According to recent estimates, 25 to 30 percent of municipal garbage is now plastic.

Recycled Plastics-Five plastic soft drink bottles make enough fiberfill for one ski jacket.[17]

Despite its questionable background, most of us have plastic products throughout our home and rarely consider how they may affect our health. Certain plastics, such as PVC (polyvinyl chloride) and plastics containing phthalates and bispenol-A, have been linked to health ailments that include reproductive problems such as early puberty, reduced sperm count, enlarged prostrates and breast cancer. [18] Two plastic substances are the most controversial. *Phthalates* are commonly found in products like food wrap, shower curtains and other plastic products that tend to be soft and malleable. The other substance, *bisphenol-A*, can be found in items like baby bottles, food can liners and compact disks. In 1998, the Consumer Product Safety Division was so concerned with the health effects of bisphenol-A that it convinced manufacturers to take bisphenol-A out of products like drinking cups and other plastic products babies put in their mouths. In 2000, the European Union considered banning PVC's from products such as food wrap, packaging and appliances, because they release dangerous chemicals when incinerated and are difficult to recycle. When manufactured, PVC is one of the largest producers of dioxin, a known carcinogen that is linked to birth defects. The EPA has determined there is no safe level of dioxin exposure. [19]

Try to avoid vinyl and PVC whenever possible. As a general rule, stay away from plastics that smell. You can tell if a plastic bottle is made from PVC if it has a #3 recycling code on the bottom. To be on the safe side, limit your overall use of household plastics, especially plastics that are soft and malleable.

What are the alternatives to plastic? Try using anything made of glass, ceramics or even wood, bamboo or coconut products. Consider using waxed paper instead of plastic wrap. These materials are much more environmentally friendly and pose less of a health risk to you and your loved ones.

Kitchen Cleaning
Cleaning up your Kitchen Chemicals

All too often we use household cleaning products without thinking twice about what they might be leaving behind: layers of chemical residue on carpets that babies crawl on; filmy deposits on furniture and countertops that make their way into our hands, into our mouths and food, and invisible clouds of indoor pollution. Is this what we really mean by a clean home?

Every year there are more and more products that claim to make our homes cleaner, brighter, whiter, germ free and perfect. Is there a way to clean our homes without adding to the chemical load we have already unleashed into our environment? By going back to some basic, natural cleaning products our grandmothers used, we can reduce both the chemical toxins and germs in our homes, while keeping our homes sparkling clean. This is also a good way to save money.

Many of us assume that just because "everyone" uses a kitchen cleaning product it must be safe. The long-term effects of many chemical laden cleaning products are not well understood. Helen D. Caldicott, M.D. of Physicians for Social Responsibility, says, *"Physicians are surprisingly uninformed about the medical complications of most toxic cleaners, sprays, paints and detergents. This subject is not an integral part of the medical school curriculum, yet most bottles of household chemicals carry the warning, 'If swallowed or inhaled, contact your physician."*[20] Manufacturers are not required to include on their labels, a list of all the potentially toxic ingredients in their product. Many chemical cleaning formulas are made with synthetic ingredients, artificial colors and fragrances, and some with powerful toxic solvents and disinfectants that can have an adverse impact on human health and the environment.

Every day, Americans pour more than 32 million pounds of household cleaning solutions down the drain; a dizzying variety of chemicals that may eventually end up in our streams, rivers and oceans.[21] Some chlorine-based products, like the all too familiar dishwashing detergents and bleach many of us use, are very toxic to the environment. Chlorine releases chloroform, a probable carcinogen, into the air as you use it. As it breaks down into the environment, chlorine creates by-products that combine with other naturally occurring organic compounds to form organochlorines. These compounds are believed to cause cells to mutate when they accumulate in the food chain. This can harm DNA and cause cancer.

Is there any way to tell how toxic a cleaning solution really is? A first obvious step is to read the label for warning signs. But remember, just because a label does not carry a warning, doesn't mean it doesn't contain substances that are toxic in large quantities or cumulatively, over time.

Kitchen Chemicals
What do warning labels really mean?

1) **Danger** (or a poison with a skull and crossbones) - This means it could kill an adult if only a tiny pinch is ingested.

2) **Warning** - This means it could kill an adult if about a teaspoon is ingested.

3) **Caution** - This means it could kill an adult if up to two tablespoons to two cups are ingested.

4) **Toxic/highly toxic** - This means it is poisonous if you breathe it, drink it, or if it gets absorbed through your skin.

How do we start limiting our use of these unwelcome toxic visitors and get a fresh clean start? The answer is simple. All you need is a paper and pen for a very short shopping list of less toxic, yet effective cleaning products.

Grandma's Basic Cleaning Arsenal
Make Your Own Natural Cleaning Solutions!
Cost: $10.00

Shopping List-What You Will Need

1) An eager spirit
2) White distilled vinegar
3) Baking soda
4) Borax
5) Lemon juice (optional)
6) Bon Ami cleaning powder (optional)
7) TSP (trisodium phosphate-optional)
8) Hydrogen peroxide (optional)
9) Spray bottle
10) Sponge and/or rag
11) Bowl and/or bucket
12) Steel scouring pad

Now that you have your brand new cleaning arsenal, how do you use it? Very simple. It may take a little bit of effort the first time, but after that, it should be easy.

Multi-Purpose Cleaning Solution
- 1/2 cup of white vinegar
- 1-quart of water
(Optional - 2 tablespoons of lemon juice)

Mix the vinegar and water together in a spray bottle. Use on floors, cabinets, countertops, and windows. Spray and wipe using a clean wet sponge or rag.

Sink, Tub, and Toilet Bowl Cleaner

- 1/2 cup white vinegar
- 1/4 cup baking soda

Mix the baking soda with the vinegar and water into a paste and scrub it on to a dirty surface. Let it sit for a few minutes and wash it off with water or use it diluted on a damp sponge. Can also be used for removing burnt material on pots and pans, and removing tea stains in cups.

Pet Stains

- Baking soda
- 1/2-cup white vinegar
- 1-quart of water

Clean up the accident, and then sprinkle the area with baking soda. Leave on overnight, then vacuum or sweep the area, and wash with a white vinegar/water solution.

Window Cleaner

- 1/2 cup white vinegar
- 1-quart of water
(Optional- 2 tsp. lemon juice)

Mix the ingredients together in a spray bottle and label. Use a crinkled sheet of newspaper or a soft cloth to clean the window.

Floor Cleaners

Tile or Linoleum Floors
- 1/2-cup white vinegar
- 1-gallon of water
(Optional-1/4 cup lemon juice)

Wood and Floor Polish
Mix one part white vinegar to 1 part vegetable oil; apply a thin coat and rub in well.

Disinfecting Cutting Boards
- White vinegar
- Water
- Lemon

Rub with a slice of lemon or a 50% vinegar/50% water solution.

For Heavy Duty Cleaning
- Borax
- Liquid soap
- Trisodium phosphate

Mix a half-cup of Borax, half a teaspoon of liquid soap, and two teaspoons of TSP (trisodium phosphate) into two gallons of water. (You can buy TSP at most paint, home improvement, and even at some large grocery stores.)

For General Disinfecting

For the most effective disinfecting around, wipe surfaces with a white vinegar and water solution, and then wipe with a hydrogen peroxide solution. (Studies have shown that this cleaning solution is even more effective than conventional cleaning solutions like bleach!)

Cleaning Mold

Check refrigerator bins, door gaskets, and drip trays as well as sink areas for mold, and use this solution or plain hot soapy water to wipe the mold away.

- White vinegar
- One teaspoon of Borax
- 1-quart of water

Mix a 50% vinegar and a 50% water solution in a spray bottle. Spray and wipe clean. Or add one teaspoon of Borax or one teaspoon of liquid soap into a quart of warm water. Add a splash of lemon juice or vinegar to cut the mold. Make sure to test this cleaning solution first, to see if it stains the surface you plan to clean.

Mold - Is it lurking in your home?

Many people don't realize that indoor mold and fungus can cause illnesses with flu-like symptoms, and are linked to a variety of health problems including headaches, dizziness, and nausea and in extremely rare cases, even death. Indoor mold and fungus occur in many different colors and on all sorts of household items including wood, vinyl flooring, paneling, leather, carpeting, tile, wallpaper and even metal. Anywhere there is moisture, darkness, food, or a lack of ventilation, mold can be present.

To avoid mold, refrain from installing carpeting in the kitchen, bathroom, basement or any other place where water can accumulate. Also, avoid vinyl wallpaper, plastics, synthetic finishes and emulsion paints, all of which are impermeable and can trap moisture causing mold growth. Keep garbage receptacles as clean as possible. Replace carpet or wood materials that are moisture damaged. Improve water drainage in areas near or under the house. Increase the ventilation in crawl spaces, remove excess debris, and cover exposed areas with plastic. If allergies persist, consider using a HEPA air filter in the bedroom or in other rooms with a musty odor. Ventilation, heating, and strong sunlight inhibit bacteria and mold growth.

For cleaning mold and other dirt, you may wonder if "Grandma's Basic Cleaning Arsenal" will really keep things clean and germ-free. Try them and see for yourself. But keep in mind that conventional cleaning products don't guarantee to leave surfaces free of disease-causing bacteria and viruses; only boiling water can do that. Even if a chemical solution could kill all germs, it would ultimately be ineffective, since microbes reproduce extremely fast and return in no time.

If you are too busy to create "Grandma's Basic Cleaning Arsenal," you can buy low toxic cleaning products from stores and catalogs. Look for products that are rapidly biodegradable, low-toxic and are not tested on animals. Remember, always store cleaning and other toxic products in a child and pet-proof cabinet or pantry.

Cookware, Dinnerware, and Containers
Dish Up the Best

Cost: Low-End Set - $50
Mid-Level Set - $50-$200
High-End Set - $200+

Cooking Pots and Pans - Cook Up a Storm

When choosing pots and pans, select those that suit your cooking style and are safe for both you and the environment. It's important to know that some materials used for cookware are more environmentally friendly and safer than others.

Non-Stick Cookware - Reduce Your Fat Intake

A great deal of new cookware is coated with a hard, non-stick surface that makes it possible to use less fat when cooking, which is a major health benefit. This type of cookware is also easier to clean and the food is less likely to burn.

The new non-stick coatings are tougher than Teflon®, the original non-stick coating that tended to flake off, and which is surrounded by health controversy. The new coatings may flake into your food with undetermined consequences, particularly if you use metal utensils. But, many people feel the benefits of non-stick coatings outweigh the risks and choose these kinds of pots and pans.

Aluminum Pots and Pans - Avoid Non-Anodized Aluminum Cookware

Aluminum cookware has always been a popular choice because it heats up fast, doesn't rust and in most cases is inexpensive. Aluminum also retains heat better than stainless steel, once the burner is off. However, aluminum cookware may have some health and environmental drawbacks. Aluminum is considered an environmental "nasty" because it requires massive amounts of energy and water to produce. Apart from plastic, aluminum requires more energy to produce than most other household and home building materials.

The second concern is over the potential health effects of non-anodized aluminum cookware. Anodizing is the process in which aluminum is chemically treated in a hot acid bath. This prevents the aluminum from leaching into food while cooking, and makes the aluminum dimensionally tough so that it will not warp at high temperatures or dent easily. According to some studies, non-anodized aluminum has been linked to a variety of health problems, including intestinal ailments, kidney disease and Alzheimer's. Although most newer aluminum cookware is anodized, it's wise to avoid buying the less expensive cookware found at discount department stores, garage sales and thrift stores that may not have been anodized.

Stainless Steel Cookware - For a Certain Cooking Style
If your cooking style includes searing meats and caramelizing food, you may want to consider stainless steel cookware, which does not have a non-stick coating. However, stainless steel cookware has more of a tendency to burn and stick, making it necessary to add more cooking oil or fat. Stainless steel cookware also creates a moister cooking environment than aluminum pots and pans.

Glass Pots and Pans - A Clear Delight
Most people underestimate how environmentally friendly glass really is. Not only is it recyclable, non-toxic and manufactured in a relatively energy-efficient way, you can watch your food cook! Glass is commonly used for lids. You can also purchase glass baking and ovenware sets.

Copper Pots - Beautiful and Efficient
Copper pots are elegant and heat up quickly and evenly like old aluminum cookware, yet there is some concern that copper may leach into food during cooking. If you decide to buy copper cookware, make sure that you buy the kind with the copper on the outside and stainless steel on the inside, so the copper won't come in contact with food. One disadvantage of copper pots is that they need to be cleaned often to remove the tarnish on the copper.

Cast Iron Pots - A Wise Choice

Cast iron pots and pans can be relatively inexpensive, durable and leave a relatively gentle "foot print" on the Earth in terms of manufacturing, and thus make a wise and wonderful cookware choice. If you want to make your cast iron pan "non-stick," season or coat the bottom with cooking oil, and let it settle on a warm burner for one hour. Then, wipe out the excess oil, leaving a thin coat. One brand of cast iron pots is *Le Creuset®*, which are coated with enamel. The beauty of this cookware is that it can go from the stove or oven directly to the table, although it is quite heavy and expensive.

Clay Cookware - Romancing the Past

Perhaps the most romantic and sustainable cookware of all is ceramic or clay, which has been used around the globe for millennia and is still very popular in places like Mexico. Primarily used as roasting dishes, these items simply break down and return to their source once they are no longer usable. This type of cookware can be found anywhere; from your local retail outlet to the farmer's market. Clay cookware is prized for its ability to keep meat moist and tender.

When shopping for this brightly colored, glazed cookware, make sure the product does not contain lead, which is hazardous to your health. Many high-end cooking stores guarantee that their glazed ceramic ware is lead-free. However, some low-end stores carry products containing lead. One way to tell if the product contains lead is to turn the piece over. If it has lead in it, it will often say on the bottom, "This product is not intended for food usage because it is poisonous." Unfortunately, a person who does not speak English may not be able to understand this disclaimer.

Porcelain Ceramic Cookware - Space Age Technology

This is a very versatile type of cookware, often referred to as Corningware® or Pyrex®. These pots, pans and baking dishes are made from materials developed from military nose cone technology. The drawback of this type of cookware is that it can chip and contaminate your food with little plastic or ceramic bits. As an alternative, you may want to consider porcelain-on-steel cookware, which is steel cookware with porcelain on the outside for looks.

Dinnerware, Glassware and Bakingware
Support Your Local Artisan

If you want to treat yourself to something truly special and Earthwise, consider buying dinnerware from a local potter at an arts and crafts store or farmer's market. Or consider buying recycled glass stemware. By purchasing locally, you help support your community's economy and avoid wasting energy on transportation. Although supporting your local artisan may be a little more expensive, consider your purchase as a kind of donation, or as voting with your dollars.

Whenever you purchase dinnerware and glassware, you should be aware of the possibility that there may be lead in these products. Lead has long been used in ceramic and glass. Most local craftspeople are aware of the possible health risks of lead and do not use it in their products, but it is harder to determine the materials in glass and dinnerware made in other countries. Products containing leaded glazes are still found on store shelves of large retailers and in craft stores. When in doubt, ask the store clerk or call the manufacturer to ask if a product contains lead, and which products have been fired at the highest temperatures. In general, the higher the firing temperature, the safer and more inert the lead will become. The highest-risk is usually found in pottery made in developing nations. Be particularly careful about products that are shiny or brightly colored. When in doubt, make sure not to store food or liquids in glass, chinaware or pottery you suspect may contain lead. If you want to be doubly sure, simple home lead-testing kits are available at your local paint or home improvement store, usually for about ten dollars.

Cutting Boards - Wood or Plastic?
Banish Those Resident Microbes

When it comes to cutting boards, the usual options are plastic or wood. What is better, a petroleum or tree product? When choosing, you should know two things: You should have two boards; one for proteins like meats, fish and cheese and a second board for bread, fruits and vegetables. This allows you to avoid contaminating the "non- protein board" with "protein-board" microbes. The second thing is that neither wood nor plastic harbors more microbes. Recent tests show that plastic boards harbor as many microbes as wooden ones. But, if a plastic or wood board has deep cuts in the surface, it should be replaced, because deep cuts can create permanent homes for harmful bacteria. A simple solution is frequent cleaning. The dishwasher does an excellent job of killing bacteria, since extremely hot water kills microbes.

Appliances
Your Ticket to Water and Energy Savings

The U.S. Department of Energy predicts that the world will use 59% more energy in 2020 than it does today.

Talking about appliances may not be the way to impress a date, but if you are interested in saving money, energy and water, learning about kitchen appliances is well worth your time.

Appliance Package Prices
Low-End Set-$2,000+
High-End Set-$12,000+

Per Unit Prices
Dishwashers-$250-$1,500+
Refrigerators-$400-$1,300+
Washing Machines-$300-$1,500+
Dryers-$200-$850+
Ranges-$300-$1,000+
Microwave Ovens-$40-$600+
Portable Convection Ovens-$179-$1,400+

Dishwashers
Save Money, Energy, and Water

**A dishwasher uses less water than hand washing
the same amount of dishes with the water running
continuously.**

If you are looking for the most energy-efficient dishwasher possible (which will also probably be the quietest) be prepared to pay a little extra. There are also moderately priced dishwashers that are reasonably energy efficient. Lower priced dishwashers often clean less efficiently because they usually lack the filters that prevent tiny bits of food from sticking to dishes.

There are several things to look for, in terms of energy and water efficiency, when comparing dishwasher models. First of all, look for the

U.S. EPA's Energy Star label. The Energy Star program awards companies whose appliances contribute to energy or water savings by reducing the amount of energy needed. Next, look inside the unit for the energy guide label that shows the machine's yearly energy

costs. Ideally, you will choose a dishwasher with low operating costs and an Energy Star label.

In addition to energy efficiency, you'll want to consider how much water a particular dishwasher consumes. A water-efficient dishwasher is one that consumes less than 6-7 gallons of water in a cycle, rather than the average 7-10 gallons. Some late-model dishwashers can be surprisingly water efficient. Using less water means using less energy as well.

Here are some other energy and water-saving tips: Avoid models with "soil sensors" that gauge how dirty the dishes are. These tend to be far less energy efficient. Try to use the lightest setting on the dishwasher. This saves money and energy. Scraping, rather than rinsing dishes before loading, saves water. If you feel tempted to do the dishes by hand, to conserve water, wash them in a container filled with soapy water instead of letting the faucet run continuously. You can also use relatively clean dish water to water your outdoor plants!

Americans and Energy Usage

The amount of energy consumed daily by one American is equivalent to that used by:

- 3 Germans
- 6 Mexicans
- 14 Chinese
- 38 Indians
- 168 Bangladeshi

-Source-Whole Terrain (2001/2002)

Refrigerators
Consider Buying a Lean and Mean Energy Efficient Machine

Want to make a big contribution to the Earth in the kitchen? Get a new refrigerator. Replacing an old refrigerator with a newer energy-efficient one is probably one of the most Earth-friendly actions you can take. *Refrigerators use $1/6^{th}$ of the electricity consumed in the U.S., or the equivalent of the energy produced by thirty giant power stations.*[22]

Investing in a new refrigerator is a win-win equation. If you select a current model with an Energy Star label (the federal government's indication that the appliance is one of the best appliances available for energy efficiency), it will cost between $35 and $70 less to run per year than the average refrigerator (circa 1985). This could add up to a total savings of $525 to $1050 during the refrigerator's lifetime - approximately the cost of the refrigerator itself. In addition, refrigerators manufactured after 2002 are made without hydro chloro-fluorocarbons, which are destructive to the Earth's ozone layer.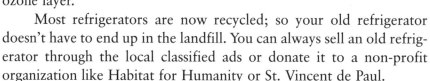

Most refrigerators are now recycled; so your old refrigerator doesn't have to end up in the landfill. You can always sell an old refrigerator through the local classified ads or donate it to a non-profit organization like Habitat for Humanity or St. Vincent de Paul.

How do you choose the right refrigerator out of the sea of possibilities? There are a few basic things to keep in mind. First, you want to choose one that is the right size, style and the highest level of energy efficiency. For starters, choose only the size you need. Larger refrigerators usually cost more and consume more electricity. Next, try to get one with the freezer on top, which is usually more energy efficient than having the freezer on the bottom or on the side. Think twice about whether you really need automatic ice and water dispensers on the front, as they require more energy to run, need special plumbing to install and tend to require more repairs. Next, consider getting a refrigerator with a *manual* defrost freezer because models with *auto-*

defrost units are more expensive to run since they have a heater. Refrigerators with manual defrost freezers, however, aren't as readily available these days. If you don't have time to defrost your freezer regularly, an automatic defroster unit is a good choice; but make sure to get the most energy efficient auto-defroster possible. Also, remember that letting ice build up in the freezer consumes a lot of extra energy.

How do you know which models are most energy efficient? Again, look for the Energy Star label. Purchasing an Energy Star model may also qualify you for special rebates from your local utility/power company or government. Ask the sales representative or call your utility/power company for details. Another way to determine the energy efficiency of a particular refrigerator is to look at the energy guide label (inside the door) that indicates how much electricity, in kilowatt-hours (kWh), a particular model uses in a year. A smaller 16 cubic-foot, 2004 model refrigerator (with a top-mounted freezer unit without an ice or water dispenser) may use no more than 394 kilowatts per year. A larger refrigerator, with a door front icemaker and other features, can use up to 727 kilowatts per year. There are many options to choose from, so selecting a refrigerator isn't that difficult once you know what you want.

Other options are water and ice filters that filter out impurities like chlorine, lead and other chemicals. You can buy these attachments for as little as $30.00, often at the same place where you purchased your refrigerator. The main drawback to filters is that they often need to be replaced once or twice a year.

Handy Dandy Refrigerator Tips
For Penny and Power Savings

1) Don't keep your refrigerator too cold. Thirty-five degrees to thirty-nine degrees F for fresh food, and five degrees F for frozen food, will be just fine. Since most refrigerators only have incremental setting dials, use a thermometer to determine the temperatures inside your refrigerator.

Handy Dandy Refrigerator Tips cont.

2) Let hot foods cool down a bit before putting them in the refrigerator. You don't want the refrigerator to work harder than it has to.

3) Cover liquids and wrap foods stored in the refrigerator. Uncovered foods release moisture, which makes the compressor work harder. Don't overload refrigerators with items that block air circulation and make the refrigerator work harder. This saves money and extends the life of the compressor.

4) Defrost your manual-defrost refrigerator/freezer on a regular basis. Don't let frost build up more than 1/4 inch. Frost build-up increases the energy needed to keep the motor running.

5) Make sure your refrigerator/freezer doors are airtight. Test them by closing the door over a dollar bill with the bill half-in and half-out. If the bill pulls out easily, the seal needs replacing or the latch needs an adjustment.

6) Move the refrigerator out from the wall and vacuum its condenser coils a few times a year unless you have a no-clean condenser model. Your refrigerator will run for shorter periods with clean coils.

7) Do not place the refrigerator next to a stove or any warm place that compromises its cooling capabilities.

8) Open and close the refrigerator as little as possible.

9) Never defrost a freezer with a knife or pick.

Washing Machines
Clean Up Your Energy and Water Act

14% of the water consumed in the average American home is used by washing machines, which use an average of 40-60 gallons of water per load.

If you are in the market for a new washing machine, consider getting one that is front-loading (a horizontal axis machine) instead of one that is top loading. Front-loaders may cost a bit more, but use one-third the energy of and less water, than a top-loading machine. Another nice thing about front-loading washing machines is that they remove more water during the spin cycle than top loaders, which will give you a good head start on drying. Many washing machines also allow you to save even more water with an extra small load feature that lets you fill the machine accordingly.

As with other appliances, look for the federal government's Energy Star label to help you find the most energy efficient models available. All washers manufactured after 2003 are required to use 22 percent less energy than 2003's least efficient models.

Dryers
Dry Up Your Energy Needs

When comparing dryer models, keep in mind that the more expensive models generally accommodate larger loads and offer a few extra conveniences, such as accurate moisture sensors and air-only cycles. Air-only cycles are a great feature that dries with cold air, saving money and energy, and helps to keep your clothes wrinkle-free. With dryers, the most efficient run on natural gas. In addition, models with a moisture sensor (that automatically shuts off the machine when the load is dry), save energy as well as reducing wear on clothing from over-drying. The one possible disadvantage of choosing natural gas, is that it requires a natural gas line, which may be costly to install if you don't have one already.

ℋandy 𝒟andy ℒaundry 𝒯ips

1) Don't over-dry the laundry. If you have a moisture sensor, use it to save energy.
2) Wash and dry your laundry with a warm or cold setting instead of a hot one.
3) Wash and dry full loads.
4) Dry heavy cottons and towels separately from lighter weight clothes.
5) To improve air circulation, clean the lint filter in the dryer after every load.
6) Use the residual heat of the dryer, by using the cool-down cycle to allow the clothes to finish drying.
7) Dry your clothes outside in the sunshine on a clothesline whenever possible.
8) Try using an indoor drying rack, which saves energy and is particularly useful for lightweight and delicate items.
9) As recommended by appliance manufacturers, make sure to replace a washing machine's rubber fill hoses every three to five years to prevent worn hoses from bursting. Replace worn rubber hoses with braided or stainless steel ones for added security.

Stoves
Get the Heat on Healthy and Energy-Efficient Cooking

Natural Gas Vs. Electric Stoves

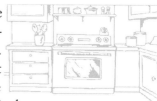

Even though they are more expensive to buy, natural gas stoves generate 40 percent less global warming carbon dioxide. One drawback to natural gas stoves is that they can produce noxious by-products like carbon monoxide, nitrogen dioxide and particulates among other pollutants in your home. Most new models have electronic ignitions, which reduces this pollution. If you have a healthy home, with a good kitchen and whole house ventilation system, this problem can be minimized. A powerful kitchen fan of at least 200-300 CFMs (cubic feet of air exchange per minute) that vents outside the house can eliminate 70 percent of all kitchen pollution. When cooking, open a window to allow fresh air to replace air being pumped outside by the fan. Activated charcoal-filter kitchen fans, often called recalculating range hoods that re-circulate air, are not nearly as effective. Another way of reducing pollution is to watch the color of the burner flames. Make sure they are blue. A yellow color indicates inefficient burning and that the gas-supply line probably needs to be serviced and cleaned. If you have a natural gas stove, especially an older model, or any other natural gas appliance, a carbon-monoxide detector is recommended in order to avert any health problems and detect possible gas-line leakage.

Handy Dandy Stove Tips

1) When purchasing a gas stove or range, try to get one with an automatic electric ignition system (rather than a continuously burning pilot light). An electric ignition system saves 41 percent of gas used in the oven and 53 percent of the gas used on the top burner. Most new models have this feature, yet many of the older models do not.

2) With gas burners, make sure the flame is small enough so that it does not spread beyond the bottom of your pan. On electric ranges, use pots that are no smaller than the diameter of the heating element.

3) Keep range-top burners and reflectors clean. This will save you energy because they will reflect heat better.

4) If you have an electric range, get in the habit of turning off the burner a few minutes before your food is done, since it takes a while for the heating element to cool. The same principle applies to oven cooking in an electric oven.

Microwave Ovens
They May be Fast, but are they Safe?

Although microwave ovens are very energy-efficient and fast, the potential health risks due to possible radiation leakage and general exposure are still inconclusive. Among some of the potential health risks associated with this kind of radiation exposure are headaches, irritability, heart and thyroid problems and even cancer. New models are much safer and sturdier than older ones. Before purchasing a microwave oven, use the most recent consumer guides to help you find the sturdiest, safest model possible. Problems with older microwaves occurred when units were dropped, banged or overused; broken seals or casements allowed radiation to leak.

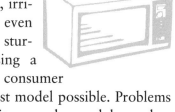

If you do have a microwave oven, make sure that you stand at least three feet away from it during operation. Keep your appliance in top operating shape by checking to make sure the oven door opens and closes properly, no food or other substances have accumulated around the door seal and no damage has occurred to the latches, hinges, sealing surfaces or door.

If you get a microwave oven, there are plenty of benefits. Most importantly, microwave ovens are a lot more energy-efficient than just about any other cooking appliance. Because they heat much faster than large electric or gas stoves, it makes them perfect for heating up small portions. When microwave cooking, it is very important to use cookware made of glass or ceramic instead of plastic, which can leach harmful substances into food while heating and may even give food a "plastic" flavor. If you decide to get a new microwave, they come in compact, medium, and large sizes; choose one that best fits your kitchen size and layout.

Portable Turbo-Convection Ovens
Fast, Efficient, and Earthwise

Using a built-in fan to circulate heat, an electric convection oven cooks without hot spots. A convection oven uses less energy than a conventional electric oven, takes 25 to 30 percent less time for cooking and cooks just as well, and sometimes even better, than a full-sized oven. Some convection ovens are also economical to purchase. The main drawback to these ovens is that they are too small to accommodate large items like turkeys. If possible, try to place a turbo-convection oven underneath the range hood or next to your stovetop, for adequate ventilation to the outdoors.

How to Recycle your Appliances
Give Your Old Appliance a New Life

The typical home appliance (stove, washer and/or dryer) contains about 75 percent steel. The good news is that, according to the Steel Recycling Institute, 84.1 percent of the appliances discarded in the U.S. in 2000 were recycled, thanks to community appliance collection efforts. If you are considering buying a more energy or water efficient appliance and are looking for a place to donate old but working appliances, try your local Habitat for Humanity at www.habitat.org, St. Vincent de Paul, or Goodwill Industries at (800)-664-6577 or www.goodwill.org. All three have reputable programs that channel old and refurbished appliances to low-income people. If your appliance is no longer in working condition, contact your local waste management facility or the Steel Recycling Institute at (800) YES-1-CAN or visit www.recycle-steel.org for information about local recycling options. Ask the local waste management company or recycler if they are licensed to remove and recycle toxic refrigerants such as Freon®, which deteriorates the Earth's ozone layer.

Kitchen Ventilation
Keep your Air Fresh and Toxin-Free

Every healthy home should have a powerful kitchen exhaust fan that eliminates indoor pollution by venting cooking fumes, chemical gases, grease, heat and moisture. The flames of gas and wood burning ranges in particular, produce burn by-products like carbon monoxide, nitrogen dioxide and other pollutants. Kitchen hood fans that do not vent to the outside and simply recirculate bad indoor air are not effective. It is important to get a fan with at least 200-300 CFM's in order for it to work effectively. This means that it exchanges 200-300 cubic feet of air per minute. Besides having a working exhaust fan, it is always good to open kitchen windows and doors as much as possible, especially on windy days when it's easier to flush out trapped toxic air. It is also beneficial to have some plants in the house because they can absorb a small bit of carbon dioxide and other gaseous toxins.

In case of a kitchen fire, be prepared. In addition to a readily accessible fire extinguisher, have a box of baking soda handy to put out grease fires.

Handy Dandy Kitchen Water Saving Tips

The average American's daily activities require the consumption of 2,000 pounds of water. [23]

1) Thaw frozen foods by leaving them on the countertop or in the refrigerator. Do not run hot water over them.
2) Before putting dishes in the dishwasher, rinse or scrape them in a pan of water in the sink. Rinsing them under running water wastes an average of 15.7 gallons per washing.

Handy Dandy Tips cont.

3) Compost your non-meat and nonfat kitchen scraps instead of using the garbage disposal. You can temporarily store your kitchen scraps on the counter or under the sink in a container about the size of a quart of milk with a lid on top to keep out insect pests.
4) Keep a glass bottle of drinking water in the refrigerator instead of running the tap until the water runs cold enough.

Chapter 4

THE LIVING AND DINING ROOMS

Thrive in Earthwise Elegance

"The human soul needs beauty more than bread."
—D. H. Lawrence

The Living Room

Create a Budget for Your Room-

ITEM	Approximate Cost
Cost Estimates-	
Sofa	$500-$4,000+
Love Seat	$400-$3,000+
Occasional Chair	$300-$2,500+
Wing Back Chair	$300-$2,000+
Cocktail Table	$150-$2,000+
End Table	$75-$1,000+
Sofa Table	$200-$2,000+
Book Shelf	$300-$2,000+
Buffet and Hutch Top	$750-$9,000+
Entertainment Center	$600-$8,000+
Desk	$250-$3,000+
Art Work (Reproduction)	$30-$700+
Art Work (Original)	$100-$4,000+

Floor Lamps	$40-$1,000+
Table Lamps	$30-$700+
Sconce Lights	$40-$1,000+
Overhead or Pendant Light	$75-$2,000+
Wallpaper	$10-$120 per roll
Paint	$15-$40 per gallon
Soft Window Treatments (drapes)	$50-$300 per average size window-(includes drapes and hardware)
Hard Window Coverings	$30-$300 per average size window (blinds and shades)

(These prices are a complete range of low, medium, and high end products. Estimating is very difficult without knowing the components for manufacture.)

Insert these furnishing prices into the 5-year Budget Planner on the following page to estimate your living and dining room decorating costs.

5-Year Budget Planner

Project	Year One Approx. cost	Year Two Approx. cost	Year Three Approx. cost	Year Four Approx. cost	Year Five Approx. cost
Walls					
Paint					
Wallpaper					
Art Work					
Mirrors					
Floors					
Carpet					
Hardwood					
Tiles					
Rugs					
Windows					
Drapes					
Blinds					
Film					
Furniture					
Sofa					
Chairs					
Ottoman					
Case Goods					
Dining Room Set					
Cabinet					
Entertainment Center					
Tables					
Lighting					
Floor Lamps					
Table Lamps					
Sconces					
Ceiling Light					
Accessories					
Pillows					
Photos					
Clocks					
Plants					
Art Work					
Yearly Total					
5 Year Grand Total					

Try to picture how you would like your living room and dining rooms to look. How do these surroundings reflect who you are? How do you feel in these rooms? What does the furniture look like? What colors do you see? In your imagination, picture the drapes, the rugs. Is there a fireplace? What type of lighting do you have? How is your furniture arranged? Together let's create a road map or sketch where only the details need to be filled in.

This chapter will guide you in creating a beautiful and functional living room and dining room in Earthwise elegance; something you'll be proud of that reflects the very best in you. It will also cover topics like choosing ergonomically-sound furniture  and how to create a sample board and a furniture floor plan.

Let's start with the floor. For living rooms, dining rooms, offices and dens, there are many gorgeous, Earthwise options. Since flooring accounts for 30 percent of a room, it's wonderful to have so many choices. These range from carpeting and rugs made from wool, recycled materials, sisal, coir (coconut), sea grass and hemp to "hardwood" flooring made from bamboo, cork, certified hardwoods and salvaged wood.

Flooring
Carpeting, Natural Reed Rugs, and "Hardwood-style" Flooring

Prices-
  Wool Carpeting-$25-$100+/sq. yd.
  Recycled Polyester (PET) Carpeting-$10-$27+/sq. yd.
  Conventional Nylon Carpeting-$15-$27+/sq. yd.
  Sisal-$26-$80+/sq. yd.
  Coir-$20+/sq. yd.
  Sea Grass-$18-$26+/sq. yd.

Hemp/Mountain Grass-$22-$30+/sq. yd.
Jute-6-by-9 area rug with finished edge, about $200+
Bamboo-$7-$9+/sq. ft.
Cork-$7-$10+/sq. ft.
Certified Wood Flooring-Depending on the type of wood and the mill it comes from, this type of wood can be competitive with standard hardwood floor prices.
Salvaged Wood Flooring-can be two to three times the price of standard hardwood floors.

Recycled Polyester and Wool Carpeting

If natural reed rugs are not your thing, and you prefer a softer, more refined or traditional look, then wool carpeting and polyester carpeting made from recycled bottles (PET carpeting) may work for you. Although carpeting made from recycled plastic bottles does not usually wear as well as traditional nylon or wool carpeting, it is generally easier to clean than traditional nylon carpeting. **(For more information on wool carpeting or PET/recycled carpeting refer to page 135 and 136.)**

Natural Reed Rugs

Unlike nylon carpeting (made of petroleum by-products), sisal and other natural reed area rugs are an Earthwise choice, provide a neutral, textured look, do not emit noxious chemicals and are made with biodegradable plant materials.

Natural reed rugs look especially fine in contemporary, northwest, southwest, Arts and Crafts and Asian style homes. They are particularly suited for homes in warmer or coastal climates since they hide sand well and have a light and airy feel. If you purchase sisal, or any other natural fiber rug, try to get one with a natural rubber or latex backing instead of vinyl (which is not biodegradable and tends to off-gas toxins). In addition, vinyl consumes huge amounts of energy in the manufacturing process.

One type of reed rug is sisal. Perhaps the most popular and strongest of the reed rugs, sisal comes from the plant *Agave sisal,* grown in managed plantations in places like Brazil, Mexico and east Africa. This plant requires few pesticides or other chemicals to grow successfully. And sisal rugs do not require complex mechanical processes to create. Like other fiber rugs, sisal provides texture in casual or elegant living room settings. However, sisal is not recommended for use in dining rooms, kitchens or bathrooms, or in a house with small children, because it stains easily, is not water resistant and tends to be rough on the feet.

Coir rugs are an alternative to sisal. Made from coconut husks, which are incredibly common and replenishable in tropical climates, coir provides an environmentally friendly, sustainable industry in impoverished, third world communities. Coir looks similar to sisal but is rougher in texture and is commonly used in doormats.

More expensive than coir, but less expensive and softer looking than sisal, sea grass fiber rugs are made from a replenishable seaweed, which grows very quickly in the ocean. Another natural fiber to consider for area rugs is jute. Jute rugs are usually less expensive than many others, yet can add a rough-hewn texture to a room.

Hemp/Mountain Grass Rugs

"The best hemp...is the first necessity to the wealth and protection of the country." - Thomas Jefferson

Hemp or mountain grass rugs are another eco-friendly possibility. Naturally mildew resistant, twice as strong as cotton and much easier on the feet than sisal, hemp looks like a cross between wool and sisal and has great potential for solving the many environmental "ills" of home furnishing. Hemp or "mountain grass" (as it's called in the furnishings industry) is a "miracle" fiber that grows amazingly fast, requires few pesticides or other chemicals and can be used in a vast array of products, including window treatments, upholstery, napkins, place mats, shower curtains, pot holders, towels, even clothes, paper and cosmetics. Hemp has the potential to replace some of the environmentally questionable timber production and much of the pesticide and fertilizer-dependent cotton industry. Hemp matures in just 120 days, while many trees take about 100 years to reach maturity.

Hemp has been around for a long, long time. The Mayan people used hemp for their shoes. The Declaration of Independence was written on hemp paper. Thomas Jefferson considered hemp and tobacco to be two of the most valuable commodities of his time. In the 1930's, the United States began to severely restrict hemp production, concerned that some farmers might hide illegal drug-grade marijuana within hemp plots. Although commercial grade hemp has an appearance similar to marijuana, it has different chemical properties. Canada, England and Germany, along with about 28 other countries, successfully grow and manufacture industrial hemp under government safeguards and licenses.

The Charm and Beauty of Hard Flooring

If you want to avoid carpeting altogether and prefer hard floors, there are many new beautiful and Earthwise options including timber bamboo, certified wood, salvaged wood, tiles, stone, and even polished concrete. One benefit of hard flooring is that it is easy to clean. Unlike synthetic carpeting, it does not have to be replaced and sent off to a landfill every ten years, it does not off-gas chemicals or serve as a sponge for all the chemicals we track in on our shoes or spray in our house. Of course, the best possible situation is to find an existing hardwood floor under that grimy old carpet that just needs to be sanded and refinished with an environmentally friendly sealant. But, if you are not blessed with this situation, you'll probably want to hire a contractor to install new flooring.

Bamboo Flooring
The New Darling on the Block

Elegant, tough, and as durable as traditional oak floors, bamboo flooring is now a hot item in design markets. Capable of growing an astonishing two feet in one day and reaching maturity in only four to six years, timber bamboo often comes from Vietnam and China, and is another home furnishings "miracle plant" like hemp, that can take the place of cutting down forests. Bamboo needs few pesticides, fertilizers or herbicides and grows beautifully on organized plantations. *This is important because it is projected that worldwide wood usage will double in the next 50 years!*

The bamboo plant has a history that is just as fascinating as its myriad uses. Used in Asia for thousands of years, the Japanese associate bamboo with spiritual qualities like strength, purity, flexibility and uprightness. Asians have used bamboo for many things, including household tools, fences and buildings. Bamboo has been popular in many places like Victorian England, where it was considered a luxury and used for screens, chairs, desks and beds.

Bamboo comes in either a light or dark shade of tan, and can be stained. The flooring is constructed by laminating strips of bamboo together to form planks, which can then be nailed, glued or floated on a sub floor. When determining bamboo quality, look at the side of the product. If the plank has non-uniform strips with no gaps, the cane was either harvested too young or too old. If the bamboo was cut down too young, it may not be hard enough for durability. You can purchase bamboo flooring either in a finished or unfinished state, lay it yourself or hire a professional to install it.

One disadvantage of bamboo flooring is that it can be scratched or dented especially by pets. Another issue is that if too much water is used when cleaning, the ends of the planks may become damaged.

Grown commercially in a controlled way on plantations, bamboo is wonderful aesthetically and ecologically.

Cork
For a Rich and Earthy Look

Rich and earthy-looking, and available in a variety of styles, patterns, and colors, cork flooring is an eco-friendly home improvement that people easily fall in love with. Made from the bark of the cork tree that can be harvested every ten years, cork looks great, doesn't rot or grow moldy and is a very effective heat and sound insulator. Cork is ideal for families with children because it is such a good sound insulator, is so warm and comfortable, and because it has a bouncy resiliency. This makes cork a good material for kitchens and yoga/meditation rooms since it is not cold like tile.

Certified Forest Hardwood Flooring
For a sustainable forest future

Another option is good old-fashioned hardwood floors. If you are not fortunate enough to have old hardwood floors that simply need refinishing, you can install them. As caring citizens, we want to purchase wood that is certified by the Forest Stewardship Council (FSC) and comes from a sustainably managed and environmentally intact forest. A sustainable and environmentally intact forest is cut selectively and in careful rotation so that healthy timber yields are realized while retaining healthy streams, and diverse plant and animal species. The best way to find FSC-approved wood is by simply calling stores to ask if they carry certified wood flooring or other such products. This might not be as hard as you might think as some very large national chain stores like Home Depot, are now starting to carry FSC approved certified wood.

**For more information about sustainable wood products,
refer to page 97.**

Salvaged Wood Flooring
Bring a Little History into your Home

Wood salvaged from demolished old buildings is now becoming popular with top architects and with those searching for a unique look. You can find this type of wood in select salvage yards and specialty lumber stores. Salvaged wood is rich in history. One stack of lumber, for instance, might come from the old growth redwood used in a Chinese warehouse that survived the 1906 San Francisco Earthquake; another stack might turn out to be the old growth Douglas Fir from a demolished baseball stadium.

However, the prices can be high. Because of salvage costs and dwindling supply, salvaged old growth and resawn lumber usually costs two or three times more than new wood. But if you are lured by the gorgeous patina, the weathered appearance and the incredible durability that you can only find in old growth, you might find it worth the price. Alternatively, if you are building with post and beam, you may find that reclaimed, resawn timber is less expensive and more beautiful than new timber.

How to Refinish a Beat up old Hardwood Floor
Make it come alive and look like new

If you are blessed to discover a beat up, vintage hardwood floor underneath an old grimy carpet, count your blessings. It is not difficult to restore old floors or even to alter or update their appearance. It may only require some "T.L.C." to make it look like new. You just have to take the time to sand the floor and apply the right finish. To avoid a dusty mess, the ideal time to do this is when you first move in, before all the furniture and other items are in place. But even if you have to move things around, refinishing can be well worth the trouble for the stunning beauty, texture and color of the finished product. The warmth and charm of hardwood floors definitely enhances the home, not to mention the value it adds if and when you want to sell.

The Sanding Procedure - Step by Step

The first thing to do when refinishing a floor, is to get a random orbit sander or vibrating sander and a protective mask from an equipment rental service. Begin by sanding the floor across the grains of the boards in one direction and then in the opposite direction. When you are finished, wipe or vacuum the floor clean of any sawdust before applying the finish. Do not leave the floor in a raw unfinished condition for very long because at this stage it is very susceptible to splintering and staining. So it is wise to have the finish ready to work with before you sand so you can apply the finish right away.

How to Select your Finish

Some synthetic floor sealants, like polyurethane, off-gas extremely toxic chemicals when first applied, but these gases abate after a short period of time. These sealants tend to be very durable and don't require frequent application. If you do choose this type of product, make sure to wear protective masks, gloves and clothing, and to ventilate the room well while applying it. In addition, stay out of the room while the product is drying, possibly for a few days. Toxicologists have found that off-gassing from petroleum-based polyurethane can cause skin and eye problems, coughing, bronchitis, reduced sperm quality, and heart disease; many of these symptoms may not occur with occasional household use but after prolonged exposure.

There are now many less toxic and organic finishes and primers made from natural resins and oils that can be used instead of polyurethane-based finishes. One of the best eco-friendly floor finishing choices is a combination of penetrating natural oils and wax, which gives a soft and satin look that will last for years. You may have to touch up high traffic areas like hallways with an occasional waxing and buffing, but you really only need to refinish floors every three to five years. Another option for hardwood floors, furniture and doors is natural liquid beeswax, which has a sweet-smelling and water resistant finish. You can also use linseed oil varnish made from flax for both floors and furniture or go with another favorite among eco-friendly renovators- OS Hardwax Oil. Natural resin shellac, which is produced by the Asian lac beetle, is also good for furniture and floors if you don't mind a high gloss finish.

If you choose to refinish a floor with shellac, keep in mind that one of its drawbacks is that it can be difficult to remove because it gums up the paper underneath the sander. Shellac also has a tendency to darken over time and is vulnerable to discoloration by water. Also, keep in mind that since shellac is alcohol-based, it is necessary to use denatured alcohol for cleaning. When applying any finish, the room should always be well ventilated. If you are refinishing a smaller furniture item, it is best done outside.

One highly recommended alternative product is called AFM Safecoat Polyseal BP. This product is extremely durable and has very low levels of VOCs. You can purchase this product from Bio Designs, the Allergy Relief Shop, N.E.E.D.S., the American Environmental Health Foundation, the Living Source and other environmental building supply stores. Another option is Crystal Aire, or an even more durable floor finish called Crystal Shield, manufactured by Pace Chem Industries, Inc., which can be used on the floors and as a sealant.

If you do not have the time or inclination to find an environmentally-friendly wood finish, it's helpful to know that some polyurethanes are less toxic than others. For example, urethane/acrylic compounds have a water-based finish, which is preferable to an oil-based finish because it contains less toxic solvents. Water-based polyurethane dries in only forty minutes and will not yellow the wood like many polyurethane finishes do. Water-based finishes also have little residual odor after less than a week, while oil-based finishes may off-gas odors for several months after application. If you have any unused finish, make sure you bring it to a toxic waste dump and not pour it down the drain where it might end up in a creek or river. Some varnishes are so toxic that there is a very high fine for dumping them down the drain.

Another type of commonly available product is acrylic finish. This product creates a hard and durable surface, but off-gases for a couple of months after application. In addition, it's extremely odorous when initially applied; quite capable of causing problems for those who are chemically sensitive.

A contractor and I were discussing the best way to get rid of toxic supplies after finishing an indoor paint job. He told me he always takes paints to the toxic dump, but that he pours varnishes and paint thinners down the drain because they are nontoxic and safe. I showed him the label on the back of a varnish can that said, "danger", a clear indication of how toxic the stuff really is, and told him about California's enormous fine for pouring the substance down the drain. Here was someone who cared enough about toxins to take them to the toxic dump, but was not informed about some of the most hazardous products.

Formaldehyde
Be Aware of this Toxic Substance Found Throughout your Home

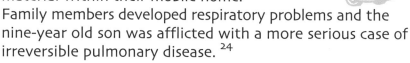

In Baytown, Texas the family of a nine year old boy was rewarded a $570,000 liability settlement for the alleged formaldehyde poisoning resulting from long-term exposure to formaldehyde off-gassing from material within their mobile home. Family members developed respiratory problems and the nine-year old son was afflicted with a more serious case of irreversible pulmonary disease. [24]

Although the manufactured home industry no longer uses urea formaldehyde foam insulation in the construction of new mobile homes, it is still commonly used in a wide assortment of home products ranging from cosmetics, to kitchen cabinets, paneling, furniture, drapes, upholstery and sub flooring.

Do you ever get little headaches or a general feeling of lethargy in the winter when the windows are closed and the heat is turned on high? What about respiratory problems? Did you ever consider that maybe the source of those unexplainable little ailments might be from the urea formaldehyde or other chemicals in your own home?

Formaldehyde is an insidious substance. It can cause headaches, dizziness, nausea, lethargy, rashes, and chronic respiratory problems, and has been labeled a probable carcinogen by the EPA. Formaldehyde may be found in many places throughout your home. It is estimated that up to twenty million Americans suffer from formaldehyde symptoms each day and don't even know it! [25]

Perhaps the most significant source of formaldehyde is pressed wood products in furniture, cabinets and even sub flooring where it is used as a binder. As much as ten percent of an average sheet of particleboard, medium density fiberboard or hardwood plywood is made up of formaldehyde that bonds the material together.[26] In fact, formaldehyde products are so pervasive that up to ninety percent of all furniture made and sold in the U.S. today is built with formaldehyde-comprised pressed wood and veneers.[27] These formaldehyde-based products can off-gas for over eight to ten years. Fortunately, there are formaldehyde-free alternatives like solid wood products, and wheat board and straw board, which are used to make kitchen and bathroom cabinets. Although the effects are still debatable, the symptoms vary and depend on exposure levels, there is no reason to risk having something that could effect your health for years to come.

Although you may not feel the risk is sufficient to warrant the time and massive expense of removing all the formaldehyde-containing products in your home, it is prudent to take steps to reduce the noxious off-gassing. One way to do this is to apply natural resin shellac on all of the surfaces of formaldehyde-containing products like cabinets and furniture surfaces. This will help seal off the formaldehyde vapors. You can also use a product like AFM Safecoat Safe Seal, which is a clear acrylic-formula finish created primarily to stop the formaldehyde off-gassing from plywood and particleboard. Also, the finish/sealant

Crystal Aire, by Pace Chem Industries is reported to reduce particle-board formaldehyde emissions by up to 92%. It also helps to open the windows and doors as much as possible to vent indoor air pollution. As Benjamin Franklin said, "...for a constant supply of fresh air...and as another means of preserving health." But, the best thing you can do is to avoid purchasing formaldehyde-containing products. Here's how:

Handy Dandy Formaldehyde Tips

1) Avoid purchasing formaldehyde-based products like synthetic-based upholstery, drapes, bedding, clothing, pressed board furniture, cabinets, paneling, sub flooring and other home furnishing items. (Be aware that product labels rarely indicate there is formaldehyde in a product.)

2) Go to an environmentally friendly building supply store to purchase sealers or formaldehyde-free products. Search on-line to find similar retailers in your area.

3) Try to purchase organic cotton, linen, silk, wool or hemp fabrics for upholstery, bedding, window treatments, table clothes, runners, napkins and clothing.

4) Purchase furniture made from FSC-certified wood.

5) Avoid purchasing pressed wood products except wheat board and other straw board products that use non-formaldehyde resin.

6) Consider purchasing furnishings made of ceramics, steel, rubber, glass, or vintage pieces and antiques.

7) If you are considering purchasing a home, think about getting an older house with original hardwood cabinets, floors, and other items that are less likely to have formaldehyde in them.

If you want to know the formaldehyde levels in your own home, test kits are available from places like Bio Designs and the American Environmental Health Foundation.

Rugs
Unify a Room with Color, Pattern, and Texture

A beautiful area rug is the perfect addition to add a splash of color, texture and pattern to a room, or to hide a blemish on the floor underneath. Soft and warm on the feet, a rug can look delightful over a cold and bare hardwood floor, can unify furniture arrangements, or divide a large room and make it feel cozier.

When shopping for an area rug, try to buy from a reputable dealer to make sure that you are getting the best quality rug for the price, and that it wasn't hand-crafted with child labor. (If you want more information on rugs and child labor consult Rugmark International at www.info@rugmark.org/about.htm.) When in doubt, ask. Try to find a rug made of natural materials like wool, silk, cotton or hemp, and if possible with a natural fiber backing like jute or rubber. Unlike synthetic nylon rugs, natural fiber rugs will not off-gas harmful chemicals, are usually made from sustainable materials and are biodegradable. If possible, try to find a vegetable-dyed rug instead of one dyed with chromium or other artificial chemicals. It will look better and fade less over the long run.

In order for a rug to "work," it needs to be the right size. Often, specialty rug stores will bring three or four out to your home so that you can see which one looks and fits the best. A general rule on rug size is that sofas and chairs should be either on or off the rug, and if the rug is in the center of a furniture grouping, there should be 8"-12" of foot space around the rug.

If you are placing an area rug over a hard surface flooring, it is best to place an underlay or padding underneath to keep it from slipping. (Sliding rugs can be dangerous.) Special underlays coated with a tacky adhesive work well for this purpose.

For information about carpeting, turn to page 135.

Rubber Flooring - Funky and Fashionable

Waterproof, tough, and flexible, rubber is a chic flooring material made from the sap of the rubber tree. It comes in a variety of dramatic colors, is available in tile or sheet form, and has an interesting texture. Natural rubber comes from rubber tree plantations in Asia and Central America. If you are going to purchase rubber flooring, make sure it is authentic and truly natural because synthetic varieties do exist. Rubber flooring does need to be sealed to prevent it from decomposing when wet.

Living Room and Dining Room Wood Furniture
Avoid purchasing unsustainable wood products

"What we are doing to the world's forests is but a mirror reflection of what we are doing to ourselves and to one another." — Gandhi

When it comes to living rooms and dining rooms, we often envision the richness of wood furniture: dining tables, entertainment centers, cabinets, coffee tables and end tables. At the same time, many of us are deeply concerned about the condition of forests in the U.S. and abroad, where irreplaceable old growth or ancient trees are cut down every day. Too often, we hear of the indiscriminate use of herbicides and pesticides, which destroy myriads of plants and insects and the common practice of replacing diverse forest ecosystems with sterile, tree farm monocultures. How can you be sure your furniture choices won't contribute to this destruction? How can you know that the dining room table you covet doesn't come from a five hundred year old  tree, or that the ramin wood coffee table you love wasn't illegally cut from a forest in Borneo full of endangered orangutans? Learning the history of different kinds of wood, buying from reputable sources and learning to ask questions about a product's history will help you make informed purchasing decisions. If our consumer-driven culture is ever going to change, we need to start asking these questions. Was this wood harvested locally? Did this wood come from an FSC-approved forest? Was it taken from old growth or from younger, smaller diameter trees? What animals live there? Was it plantation-grown? Answers to these questions help us make informed decisions.

One of the most promising ways of determining if furniture comes from an Earth-friendly source is through an internationally known wood certification program called the Forest Stewardship Council or FSC. Based in Oaxaca, Mexico, the FSC has affiliated organizations throughout the world, including the Smart Wood Program in Vermont and Scientific Certification Systems in California. These programs rigorously monitor the forestry and logging operations of timber companies that want to apply for certification that assures their eco-friendly status. Criteria for certification includes the health of nearby streams, the quality of the forest's biodiversity, its sustainability as a timber source and the quality of the local community's involvement in the timber business-all for generations to come.

So far, the FSC program has made significant strides certifying over 103 million acres all over the world. In North America alone, over 21.4 million acres have been approved for certification. Perhaps the most impressive thing about the certified wood program is that it is beginning to be embraced by some very large, mainstream companies including Home Depot, Smith and Hawken, Neil Kelly, Ikea Furniture and Anderson Windows; all of whom have agreed to carry certified wood products. So next time you shop for things like furniture, flooring, windows, carpentry wood or kitchen cabinets, remember to ask if these products are made from FSC certified wood.

Unfortunately, a recklessly managed forest can be devastating to local human communities as well as to the area's flora and fauna. One example is about the giant tropical island of Borneo, in Indonesia, which is the source of a substantial amount of the beige-colored ramin wood used in the United States for things like tables and chairs. In just a decade, over half of Borneo's ancient rain forests have been harvested, much of them illegally, destroying prime habitat for one of the most critically endangered primates, the orangutan.

Teak wood is another hardwood with a sullied past. In the 1970's, when teak furniture was extremely popular, teak forests were razed indiscriminately at a voracious rate in Thailand and other places, and often replaced with monoculture tree farms, housing developments, or hotels. Now, with very few natural teak forests left in the world, most teak furniture is made from wood grown on domesticated plantations in countries like Costa Rica.

What can you do to make sure you are not buying wood products from poorly managed forests? In general, try to avoid products made from threatened tropical woods such as rosewood, non-plantation-grown teak, non-plantation grown mahogany, ebony, ramin wood, and Brazilian cherry. Given the uncertainties, what types of wood products are more likely to be Earth-friendly? While it is usually better to use domestic rather than imported wood, the most important thing to consider is whether the wood was harvested in an ecological fashion.

░░░

Inside Story
The Evolving Consumer

As consumers, we have to start asking,
"Where did this come from?"

When shopping, never hesitate to ask. It may take a little courage, and may elicit all sorts of reactions, but it is definitely worth the effort. I had an interesting experience when shopping for a headboard one day. After combing the whole show room looking for a headboard in a certain style and price category, I zoomed in on one that especially took my fancy-an elegant and sleek Mediterranean-style wood headboard. Even though it was the best looking headboard there, I hesitated, because the wood looked suspiciously like a species that's over harvested. I asked the two sales people what kind of wood it was and where it came from. After a little research, one salesman came back and told me it was tropical wood from Asia. At that point, I was sure it was ramin wood-an environmental no-no in my book. So I told the salesman I was not interested and explained why. As I spoke, he looked very empathetic, his eyes were soft and his body posture open, making it clear that he understood my concern and perhaps even respected me for pointing it out.

On the other hand, his colleague clearly thought I was some strange creature. "You mean to tell me you don't want to buy that headboard because of that?" he said, as if I was crazy. Instead of reacting in anger, I calmly pulled out my credit card, purchased a locally-harvested pine wood bed and went on my merry way, knowing that I had done a good thing. As a footnote, I should add that the next time I went back to the store, both sales people greeted me with warmth and appreciation.

🔲🔲🔲🔲🔲🔲🔲🔲🔲🔲🔲🔲🔲🔲🔲🔲🔲🔲🔲🔲🔲🔲🔲🔲🔲🔲🔲🔲🔲🔲🔲🔲🔲🔲🔲🔲

Now that you know that many wood products may have environmentally checkered backgrounds, what are your options? There are many. For starters, you might want to consider choosing furniture made of bamboo, wrought iron, ceramic, tile, stone, steel, glass, reed or certified wood products. Try avoiding anything made of vinyl, plastic, or aluminum, which consume a lot of energy and/or water in production and are not biodegradable.

Also consider the possibility of antique or vintage pieces. Sometimes you can find something wonderful but off-colored at a garage or estate sale that just needs to be repainted, refinished or needs new door handles. By buying vintage or antique furniture, you'll have much more of a unique look (often for less money) and you'll be practicing recycling in its truest form!

Handy Dandy Tips
How to touch up old used and vintage furniture

1) **Water Rings:** Rub marks with salad oil, mayonnaise, or toothpaste, and then gently wipe off with a soft cloth. Or try heating up a thick cloth with an iron and then applying it over the stain area.

2) **Spilled Dry Paint:** Soak the painted area in boiled linseed oil, then remove the softened paint with a putty knife. If there is still residue left, rub the effected area with a boiled paste of linseed oil and rottenstone (a limestone-based furniture polish.) Then, wipe dry and repolish the area.

Handy Dandy Tips cont.

3) **Heat Marks:** Rub extra-fine steel wool or a steel wool soap pad along the wood grains.

4) **Spill-Soaked Newspaper or Magazine:** Soak the degraded area with salad oil, wait five minutes, then remove with an extra fine steel wool pad.

5) **Blemishes on Darker Woods:** Try using paste shoe polish, or a wood stain marker from a hardware or furniture store.

6) **Unpleasant Odors:** If your garage sale find smells as old as it looks, try airing it out by placing the piece outside in the shade where it is warm and dry. You can also spritz baking soda or talcum powder on it to mask musty odors or place charcoal briquettes in a pan in one of the drawers.

Inside Story
Mike-The Eco-Friendly Furniture Maker

When traveling Highway 26 on the way up to Mt. Hood in Oregon, if you are quick, you might spot the Forest Furniture Store on the right, in the tiny pine tree and log cabin-lined town of Welches. It's a Hansel and Gretel style, moss-covered wooden shack with a colorful, hand-painted wooden sign in front. When you open the door, if you are lucky, you'll catch the owner, Mike Martinez, in action; sitting on a wooden bench with nail gun in hand and alder tree branches in his lap, bending branches to and fro with large caring hands to make a beautiful wooden chair. If he's not in when you arrive, he's probably out along a nearby, misty pine-covered riverbank bending and cutting lovely green alder branches for tomorrow's furniture project.

Yes, he's off the beaten track and you probably will never be able to find Mike's gorgeous furniture at a regular store although you might find his furniture in a fine arts and crafts gallery. But, if you have a sense of adventure, you can find him where he crafts his elegant, spiraling twig furniture and purchase it on the spot.

What makes his twig furniture so eco-friendly? It is hand crafted and sold locally, not trucked across the country in gas-hogging trucks. Also, it's made out of easily renewed materials; Mike is not cutting down giant trees, he's just giving the alder trees a trim. His furniture is made without toxic chemicals found in most of today's pressed board furniture. And finally, his furniture is biodegradable. Eventually, when it falls apart, the branches can simply return to the Earth. Yes, Mike the twig furniture man is doing a good thing!

Bamboo, Rattan, and Natural Fiber Furniture
Light, Airy, and Natural

Light, airy, durable, and stain resistant, furniture made out of bamboo, rattan, sea grass and other reed materials comes from replenishable sources, are relatively nontoxic, and are biodegradable. This furniture also tends to be very durable, economical, and does not stain easily.

When considering furniture made from these materials, try to find out if it was grown on a sustainably managed plantation. Even though rattan is a replenishable item, it has been over-harvested in recent years. You'll have to make your choices carefully since most furniture does deplete natural resources making it difficult to find anything that is really truly one hundred percent eco-friendly.

Sofas and Chairs
Comfortable, Cushy, and Earthwise

Your best choices for eco-friendly upholstery for chairs and sofas are natural materials, like canvas, cotton and organic cotton, hemp, hessian (made of jute and hemp), wool, linen and silk. These materials are comfortable, elegant, biodegradable, and tend not to off-gas many toxic chemicals. Ideal furniture fillings include down, wool, flock (made from a cotton byproduct) or a feather/ down mix.

Even though you may have to purchase furniture with some synthetic fabric in it to increase its durability, it is best to avoid one hundred percent synthetics since they can off-gas harmful chemicals, are not biodegradable, and were probably manufactured using excessive amounts of energy.

Slipcovers and Reupholstery for Chairs and Sofas
Save Money and Resources

Rather than purchasing an entirely new sofa or chair, you can reupholster or place a slipcover over an existing one. With a soft, flowing and elegant look, slipcovers are an increasingly popular and inexpensive alternative to brand new furniture. Why throw out a perfectly good piece of furniture when you can change its look completely with new fabric? If you find the right eco-friendly furnishings catalog, you may be able to find beautiful slipcovers in organic cotton, hemp, hessian (made of jute and hemp) or linen.

Slipcovers need not be very expensive, can be machine-washed, (rather than dry-cleaned) and thus helps save precious resources. Add a few stunning patterned pillows to custom tailor it to your personal style, and if you ever get tired of the look, you can simply change the pillows.

If you really want a unique look, you can have an upholstery shop custom make you a slipcover or recover the whole chair or sofa. Custom-made upholstery will probably be a lot more expensive, but gives you the widest possible fabric selection.

Choosing an Ergonomically Sound Chair or Sofa
Looks aren't everything!

The last thing you want, is to buy a beautiful chair or sofa, take it home and discover that it is uncomfortable and strains either your back, neck, shoulder or buttocks. When shopping for chairs and sofas, you want to find pieces that are not only beautiful, comfortable, and eco-friendly, but are also ergonomically sound, meaning that they will not strain or put your body in pain.

The most important thing about sitting in a chair or sofa is to make sure it keeps your spine straight. Feeling relaxed and slouching anytime while sitting is not true relaxation, since you are actually making your body work much harder by straining it. Therefore, it is important to buy furniture that promotes good posture.

How do I know if that gorgeous chair I am eyeing is good for my posture? To begin with, the back of the chair should support the whole length of the spine as well as the head, and the seat should be firm enough to prevent slumping when the spine sags into a " banana" shape. The seat should not be so high that your feet dangle off the ground or so low so that the only place to sit is crossed legged. When sitting down, your hips and lower spine should be at a ninety-degree angle so that your spine stays straight. When sitting at a table or desk, make sure the table is not too high or too low. You should not be leaning forward too much or slouching. If your chair is too low, reaching up may strain your neck and shoulders.

Living Room Lighting
Light up your activities with style and energy efficiency

The living room is the hearth or the center of the home. It sets the stage for a wide spectrum of moods and activities-from the quiet, relaxing and the contemplative, to the lively and energetic. A lighting plan that mingles the delights of light and shadows, beauty and function can enhance all these activities, whether it's spending an evening reading or entertaining friends and family.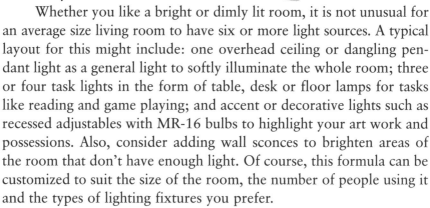

Whether you like a bright or dimly lit room, it is not unusual for an average size living room to have six or more light sources. A typical layout for this might include: one overhead ceiling or dangling pendant light as a general light to softly illuminate the whole room; three or four task lights in the form of table, desk or floor lamps for tasks like reading and game playing; and accent or decorative lights such as recessed adjustables with MR-16 bulbs to highlight your art work and possessions. Also, consider adding wall sconces to brighten areas of the room that don't have enough light. Of course, this formula can be customized to suit the size of the room, the number of people using it and the types of lighting fixtures you prefer.

When installing lighting, try to incorporate compact fluorescent light (CFL) or halogen bulbs to save money, energy, time and eventually space in the landfills. (You can get CFL bulbs for most fixtures.) Despite the relatively high start-up cost of replacing all your incandescent light bulbs with CFL bulbs, you will most likely save many times that cost in just a few years, and have the added benefit of knowing you are being an "energy-wise" citizen.

For more information on energy efficient lighting refer to p. 126.

The Dining Room

Create a Budget for Your Room

ITEM	Approximate Cost
Cost Estimates-	
Dining Room Table	$350-$3,000+
Dining Room Chair (Side)	$35-$600+
Dining Room Chair (Arm)	$35-$650+
Buffet and Hutch Top	$750-$9,000+
Cabinet	$800-$9,000+
Art Work (reproduction)	$30-$700+
Art Work (original)	$100-$4,000+
Mirrors	$50-$1,500+
Chandelier or Pendant Light	$75-$2,000+
Sconce Lights	$40-$1,000+
Table Lamp	$30-$700+
Carpeting	$15-$100+/sq. yd.
Area Rug 5' by 8'	$300-$1,500+
Wallpaper	$10-$120 per roll
Paint	$15-$40 per gallon
Soft Window Treatments (drapes)	$50-$300+ per average size window (includes fabric and hardware)
Hard Window Coverings	$30-$300+ per average size window (blinds and shades)

Dining Room Lighting
Lighting for delicious food and delightful conversation

Planning a lighting scheme for a dining room is usually simpler than for a living room. It often only requires a ceiling light, wall sconces and perhaps a little candlelight. By installing a dramatic hanging pendant light over your dining area that is at least 12" narrower than the table with a dimmer switch, you will illuminate expressive faces, mouth watering food and a lovely creative table setting. Make sure that the chandelier or pendant fixture does not block sight lines across the table or access to the table for serving or clearing a meal. The bottom of the fixture should be 30" to 36" from the top of the table.

Wall sconces provide ambient light that will add a soft and glowing dimension to the room, and illuminate areas of the room that aren't bright enough. If you have glass-fronted cabinets, you may want to consider lighting the inside of your china cabinets. Also, think about adding adjustable accent lights to highlight art work or plants. As a final touch, tall beeswax or tapioca wax candles (without lead wicks), will add mystery and ambiance to the room.

Pasting Up a Color Board (Sample Board)
Get a Sneak Preview of the Room!

Designing a color/sample board can be one of the most exciting and satisfying activities in room design because it is where all your room elements come alive for the first time. A sample board is a poster board display of all the colors, fabrics, wood finishes, and photos of possible furnishing and accessory options you would like in your room. It includes the samples of fabrics you might want to use for upholstery, a display of possible colors and textures for carpeting and window coverings, and the paint swatches and finishes for your walls, ceiling and moldings, and finishes for your furniture. The beauty of a sample board is that once you've collected all the samples, you can eliminate any that do not quite fit in with the others and make substitutes before making your final purchases.

When creating a sample board, try to display the elements in the same proportions they will be used in a particular space. For example, if you are planning on purchasing a blue carpet, make sure that it represents one third of the total board, which is probably close to the proportion it will be in the room. If you would like to add a small accessory, make sure that you show its relative size. Also, make sure you have a fabric sample large enough to reflect the true pattern or texture of the fabric you are displaying. If your plan doesn't create the room of your dreams, you can easily rearrange, add color, texture, or patterns before making a final decision. It is also good to take photos of the furniture and other design elements you would like to have in a particular room and glue those on to the poster board as well. If you want to make duplicates to show to other people or contractors, it is easy to make color copies.

What you will need to make a color/sample board:

1) Several sheets of 16" x 20" cardboard poster board in gray, green, khaki, or dark blue. (White or beige can distort colors.)
2) Scissors
3) Paste, rubber cement, or double sided tape
4) Black pen (For writing the fabric or paint name, number, source and price under each cutting and the room title at the top of the board.)
5) Fabric and paint sample swatches and basic information about all the fabrics, paints, and possible wallpaper you would like in the room.

Furniture Arranging
The Furniture Floor Plan - A Design Map You Can't Live Without!

Did you ever walk into a room and realize something was not quite right and were not able to put a finger on what it was? There's a good chance the room was suffering from a lack of a furniture floor plan. A furniture floor plan is one that determines the best choice and arrangement of furniture and other design elements to create a room that is both spatially balanced and functional. Everyone in the room should feel comfortable doing what they love best, whether it is reading, socializing, working, movie watching or game playing.

A furniture floor plan is a bird's eye view of the room looking down on the room as if there wasn't a roof. By outlining the space to the exact dimensions of the room, and drawing the furniture and other design elements to scale, a floor plan will help you understand how the room will function, and how much space will be available for various furnishings and activities. A floor plan will show you if there is extra room for a desk, dining table or seating arrangement. If the room seems crowded on paper, it will probably feel crowded in real life. A floor plan can help you avoid costly and time-consuming mistakes.

Often it's not the furnishings, but how they are arranged or placed, that makes a room come alive, look beautiful and comfortable. Even the most elegantly furnished room can look and feel off-balance if it is not properly laid out.

Trying to design a room without a furniture floor plan is one of the most common yet preventable decorating mistakes. Without a plan you may end up with too much furniture in a room, making it difficult to move around and feel cluttered and claustrophobic. You may end up with mostly vertical or horizontal furniture, which can look bland and uninteresting; it is best to have a balance of the two.

A furniture floor plan can help you combine rectangular and curving lines to create an interesting balance in the room. For instance, if you have mostly rectangular or boxy furniture, it helps to add some curved elements like an oval area rug, wall accessory or coffee table. One example of combining different forms is to place a circular mirror over a rectangular sideboard.

For professional and amateur alike, a furniture floor plan is essential for unifying a room and making it flow. Here are some tips to make sure your room is properly laid out, and works for you.

Handy Dandy Furniture Arranging Tips

1) Try to avoid lining up all your furniture along the walls. You do not want to create a military barrack. It is usually more appealing to float furniture like sofas and chairs away from walls in small groupings.

2) To avoid an unbalanced look, try not to position all the large vertical pieces on one side of the room.

3) Take a tape measure and a copy of your floor plan, window treatment measurements, and any other measurements with you when shopping for new items. (Keep those measurements and photos of the room in an envelope in your car glove compartment or purse.)

4) Include measurements of interior and exterior doorways and stairs to make sure any new furniture will fit into the house!

5) Allow room for foot traffic around the front door and throughout the main activity areas. It should be easy to walk to all the major furniture groupings and to perform routine tasks like watering plants or picking out music CD's.

6) Make sure there is sufficient room to walk between all furniture pieces. (A major pathway should be 3-4 feet wide.)

Handy Dandy Tips cont.

7) Do not place furniture or rugs over ventilating and heating ducts where they might be damaged or pose a fire hazard.

8) Make sure all areas of the room are sufficiently lit and that lighting levels can be adjusted to suit a particular mood or activity. Lights can be turned off to save energy.

9) Make sure to place the appropriate furniture near electrical outlets. You do not want electrical cords stretched out across the floor.

10) Avoid placing large bulky furniture in a small, low-ceilinged room. This type of furniture is more appropriate for larger rooms.

11) Reduce the clutter of incidental pieces. Do you have too many end tables, cabinets, or carts? Consider using one multifunctional piece to take the place of two or three.

12) Do you have too many chairs? Can some of those chairs be moved into another room or hallway? What about placing a couple of chairs behind a desk, console table or grouping several chairs around a table to make a game or afternoon tea table?

13) Is there too much unused or unbalanced negative space? Why not create another subdivision, which would be like another room with furniture in it? Maybe add a table with chairs or an area with a collection of tall plants.

How to Draw a Furniture Floor Plan-
What you will need:

1) Graph paper (It should have 1-inch squares divided into eighths. Two of these 1/8 squares will equal 1 foot, and one 1 inch square will equal 4 feet.)
2) Sharpened pencil and eraser
3) Ruler
4) Retractable tape measure for measuring the room and existing furniture.

How to Draw a Furniture Floor Plan for a Living Room

With a well-sharpened pencil, draw the perimeter of the room to scale on graph paper. Even though the plan on paper will be much smaller than the physical house itself, the proportions will be the same. This means that everything is made smaller on paper so that 1/4-inch on paper equals 1 foot of actual physical house structure. Next, in the same scale, draw the measurements of fixed items like fireplaces, windows, vents, radiators, unusual architectural features and power/telecommunication outlets. Make several copies of this skeleton layout. You can then draw several floor plans with different furniture arrangements and select the one that works best.

Now that you are almost ready to start designing your room, you need to identify the main focal point, which is usually the most dramatic and eye-catching thing in the room like a fireplace, window or favorite art piece. If the room lacks a focal point, you can create one by purchasing something like an area rug, piece of artwork, entertainment center etc.—something that really stands out. Once you have identified your focal point, you might want to arrange the conversation area furniture facing this so that those who spend time in the room will appreciate its uniqueness and beauty.

Next, measure your existing furniture and possible future furniture purchases. On another sheet of graph paper or even on a sticky post-it note pad, draw and cut out a template of each of these pieces drawn to the same scale as the room. By placing these furniture templates on the graph paper room, you can experiment with how you would like the room to look. At this point, don't think in terms of style but about comfort, practicality and scale. Lay out the larger pieces first because the places they can go are limited. You may want to consider having one or more of these large pieces face the focal point. Next, place the other furniture elements in the conversation area at a distance of no more than 6-8 feet apart. After that, you can fill in the other furniture pieces in the room. Make sure that every seat has an end table or a table surface within a comfortable arm's reach.

When arranging these furniture templates, keep these things in mind.

1) Can people move around easily?
2) Are furniture widths and heights varied so the room will look balanced?
3) Will this room look beautiful and comfortable?
4) Will this room be functional?
5) Is there enough space between furniture items?
6) Have you placed the furniture where it will not get too much sun, heat, or be too drafty?

After you have arranged these symbols in a complete furniture floor plan, make a copy of this design. Repeat this process again and again on another piece of graph paper for as many times as you have ideas for different furniture arrangements. After you have tried out several different layouts, select the one you like best. This will be your master design plan!

*Tip-If you don't want to do all this by scratch, there are floor plan kits you can buy that include erasable graph paper and ready-to-cut furniture templates. If doing this all yourself doesn't appeal to you, you can hire a professional interior designer who will do it for you.

What are My Window Treatment Choices?

For many people, choosing the right window treatments is one of the most frustrating decorating projects with too many choices and too many measurements. Yet, with a little bit of research, the task can be a lot easier.

When deciding on window treatments, bear in mind such features as light and privacy, how the room is used, and how sunlight filters in throughout the day. Also decide if you would like to block out light for sleeping purposes, make your home more energy efficient or protect fabrics and art work from sun damage. There are window treatments and materials that can do all this and more.

Bamboo and Woven Reed Shades

With an earthy and textured look, natural reed fiber shades offer an economical and eco-friendly alternative to their synthetic cousins. Reed fibers, especially bamboo, are also fast growing and biodegradable. Woven shades allow a subtle amount of light to filter through, and can be raised up and down to block light and to provide privacy. These shades are best cleaned or dusted with a vacuum.

If possible, stay away from vinyl and aluminum blinds, because they require massive amounts of energy and water to make, and simply don't look as attractive or interesting as other blinds and shades. Metal blinds are also poor insulators because they conduct valuable heat to the outside in the winter and encourage heat to come in during the summer.

Honeycomb Shades (Cellular Shades)
Blanket Your Windows with Insulation and Good Looks

These simple shades, which have clean lines and are easy to use, are designed for energy insulation and privacy. If you use honeycomb shades to block out drafts, you won't need to crank up the heat or spend a fortune on energy bills. In the summer, cellular shades block the sun and heat keeping your home cool and comfortable. The honeycomb cells are pockets of layered fabric that trap interior heat and prevent it from escaping. Honeycomb shades with two or three layers of pocketing are ideal. One layer does not provide enough insulation.

Try to select shades in a neutral color like white or beige. This will give you more flexibility for future design changes (and will be more acceptable to prospective buyers of your home). You will be pleased to discover how easy honeycomb shades are to use, and how durable and relatively inexpensive they can be. These shades can be cleaned with a vacuum. Honeycomb shades are a *"yes, yes, yes"* in any energy efficient home!

Solar Shades and Window Film Shades
Other Energy Efficient Shades

To make extra large windows energy efficient, woven mesh solar shades, window film or window film shades are a good choice.

Mylar window film shades are more transparent than honeycomb shades so they won't block your view. Depending on the version you select, window film can also reduce glare, fabric fading and prevent your room from heating up in the summer time. Window film and window film shades have the same effect as putting sunglasses on your windows.

Woven mesh solar shades also come in a variety of neutral color combinations that work well with any other window treatments and window trim. The beauty of these treatments is that although they block the sun, you can still see through them. These shades are made of fiberglass and have a 25% openness factor.

Measuring for Blinds, Shades, and Verticals
Would you Rather Measure Twice and Order Once, or Measure Once and Order Twice?

Now that you have an idea of what kinds of hard window treatments you may want, here are some guidelines for measuring your windows.

With a retractable measuring tape and a pen and paper, measure each window in each room from left to right. If you want your treatments mounted on the inside of your windows, measure width first and length second. Start at the top, then measure the middle, and then the bottom of the window in three different places. Make sure you do this two or three different times to avoid mistakes. If you find that some measurements vary from top to bottom because the windows are not squared properly, use the smallest horizontal dimension when ordering an inside mount. All measurements should be measured down to the nearest 1/8th inch. When measuring vertically from top to bottom, use the largest length measurement. This will block out the "light gap" and will help to further insulate the room.

Likewise, if you install a hard window treatment on the outside of the window frame, typically, the blind should be extended about 1.5 inches on each side of the window opening, although this amount can vary depending on the product. If the window has a sill, use the measurement of the windowsill width outside of the frame. If you have any other questions, the window treatment store salesperson should be able to help.

Soft Window Treatments - Glorify your Windows with Color and Texture

Draperies for Cold or Drafty Rooms-Make Your Room Warm and Cozy

If your room tends to be cold and drafty or if you live on a street, you may want to choose heavy interlined window treatments made of thick fabric like velvet or canvas. Better yet, consider adding an extra layer with honeycomb, roller or Roman shades for added insulation and privacy. For energy efficiency and draft reduction, use a thick drape material long enough to cover windows and doors and anywhere else where there may be air leakage. Since 25% of warm or cool air is lost through the windows, it is a good idea to line your drapes. This will also give the fabric more body and protect it from fading.

Draperies for Sunny and Warm Rooms
Don't Let Your Room Turn into a Beach

If your room faces south or west and gets too much direct sun or heat, avoid using fragile drapery fabrics like silk or bright colors that will fade or deteriorate rapidly. Also consider cutting back on the light by installing translucent shades or a second layer of light drapes underneath the heavier ones. But if you feel your room needs more light and sun, opt more for lighter, sheerer fabrics that will create an airy spacious feel.

With drapes or soft window treatments, you have three choices. You can buy them ready-made, you can have them custom-made or you can make them yourself.

If you want to design your own window treatments, you have plenty of eco-friendly possibilities. Among the many possibilities for fabric are vintage pieces from antique or thrift stores, or quilts and saris that can be transformed and recycled into something truly unique. Other good natural fabric choices are hemp, organic cotton, linen, ramie or silk. You can purchase these ready-made or you can make them yourself.

If you prefer not to make your own drapes, you can buy them from either a retail store or catalog. Have a picture of your window and room and the window measurements on hand to help you and the salesperson figure out exactly what you need.

Measuring for Drapes and Soft Window Treatments

Measuring for drapes or soft window treatments is a bit different than measuring for hard window treatments. One of the things you may want to do with soft window treatments is enhance the apparent size of the window. It is usually best to hang drapery panels outside of the window casing to expose as much of the window as possible. Extending the drapery as much as two feet on either side of the window with panels touching the edges of the window is not unusual. Doing this will enhance your view and make your window seem larger.

If you want the window and room to look larger, install the curtain rod as close to the ceiling as possible and let the window treatments drape generously so they hang one inch off the floor. This will create a lush and luxurious look, and the long thick curtain fabric will act like a blanket on the window helping to make the house warm, cozy and energy efficient.

You may also want to install curtain tie-backs that will allow you to pull the drapes back during the day, to let the heat and light in, and close them at night for insulation and privacy.

Fireplaces - Icons of the Past

Natural Gas Fireplaces and Stoves for Beauty, Warmth, and Energy Efficiency

Cost: *Gas fireplace insert-$1,050-$2,000*
Installation-$600-$800
Gas Log Sets-$250-$450
Installation-$400-$600

For hundreds of years, the hearth or fireplace has been the center or heart of the home. Originally, the fireplace was the source for warmth and cooking but as houses modernized, fireplaces remained an asset for extra heat and as both a social and architectural focal point. Yet for many, fireplaces still represent our deepest yearnings for warmth, belonging and security where family and friends gather to tell stories and bask in each other's company. But now times have changed; there are many more people, fewer trees and chimney smoke is a sign of pollution, not prosperity.

While wood burning fireplaces may no longer fit into our definition of a healthy home and environment, it is possible to still have the look, feel and warmth of a traditional fireplace by installing a natural gas fireplace insert, which also saves money and energy. Current natural gas fireplace inserts are much more attractive than earlier versions and offer a choice of simulated tree species for your natural gas fire "logs".

What do you need to know when shopping for a natural gas fireplace? First, you need to decide if you simply want an insert for your existing fireplace or if you want a ready-made gas unit that will be vented through your existing brick chimney or metal piping. If you want your natural gas fireplace or stove to function as a significant heat source, be sure to check it's Annual Fuel Utilization Efficiency Rating (or AFUE), which means that the unit is rated as a furnace. A unit without an AFUE rating is usually intended more for decoration, although it will still create some heat. Also make sure that the fireplace hot stove is approved by an independent, reputable testing agency like the American Gas Association.

You will be pleased to discover how energy efficient heating with a natural gas fireplace or stove really is. If you heat only the room you are using with a natural gas fireplace or stove, instead of heating up the whole house, your monthly energy bill will drop dramatically.

If you are considering getting a wood-burning stove, try getting either a new one, or a used one that was built after 1990. Newer models that have been certified by the Environmental Protection Agency release up to 75% fewer emissions than older ones. For a cleaner and brighter energy future, natural gas fireplaces and some wood stoves, are the way to go.

If you prefer the natural look and feel of a traditional fireplace or wood stove, here are some tips for making your traditional fireplace more Earth-friendly.

Handy Dandy Fireplace Tips

1) Use it sparingly and don't depend on it as a primary heat source. Fireplaces are very inefficient heat providers.
2) Burn baby burn. When you use it, make it as hot as possible. This will burn up more of the pollutants like carbon monoxide and nitrogen dioxide and particulates that will either pollute your home or the outside air. Your chimney will also stay cleaner longer.
3) Use hard wood instead of soft wood species. Even though soft wood like pine and poplar make good kindling, or starter fuel, hard wood like oak burns longer and hotter.
4) Have a chimney sweep inspect your fireplaces annually or after every cord of wood burned, ideally by a chimney sweep who is certified by the National Chimney Sweep Guild. He or she will look for cracks in the mortar, for possible deterioration of the chimney and its liner, as well for signs of animals, and will make the repairs needed to prevent fires.
5) Consider getting a chimney cover or cap to protect the chimney from being damaged by precipitation and to keep animals out.
6) Protect your home and children by using a fireplace screen to prevent sparks from landing on the furniture and floor.
7) Make sure everyone in your home, especially children, understands basic fire safety. Keep screens closed, and hands, clothing, toys, etc. away from the fire. Never leave a smoldering fire unattended.
8) Keep a fire extinguisher in the home, and make sure everyone knows how to use it.

❀ ❀ ❀

Chapter 5

THE BEDROOM

Sleep Soundly and Wake Up Invigorated

"The bed, my friend is our whole life.
It is there that we are born,
it is there that we love, it is there that we die."
—Guy de Maupassant

Create a Budget for Your Room

ITEM	Approximate Cost
Headboard/Footboard	$300-$4,000+
Night Stand	$75-$2,500+
Dresser	$350-$4,000+
Art Work (reproduction)	$30-$700+
Art Work (original)	$100-$4,000+
Mirrors	$50-$1,500+
Table or Swing Arm Lights	$40-$700+
Sconce Lights	$40-$1,000+
Overhead or Pendant Light	$75-$2,000+
Carpeting	$15-$100/sq. yd.
Area Rug 5' by 8'	$300-$1,500+

Wallpaper	$10-$120 per roll
Paint	$15-$40 per gallon
Soft Window Treatments (drapes) (includes drapes and hardware)	$50-$300+ per average size window
Hard Window Treatments (blinds and shades)	$30-$300+ per average size window

(These prices are a complete range of low, medium, and high end products.)

Insert these furnishing prices into the 5-year Budget Planner on the following page to estimate your bedroom decorating cost.

5-Year Budget Planner

Project	Year One Approx. cost	Year Two Approx. cost	Year Three Approx. cost	Year Four Approx. cost	Year Five Approx. cost
Walls					
Paint					
Wallpaper					
Art Work					
Mirrors					
Floors					
Carpet					
Hardwood					
Tiles					
Rugs					
Windows					
Drapes					
Blinds					
Shades					
Furniture					
Loveseat					
Chair					
Ottoman					
Case Goods					
Headboard/Footboard					
Night Stands					
Armoire					
Dresser					
Lighting					
Swing Arm or Table Lamps					
Recessed Lights					
Sconces					
Ceiling Light					
Accessories					
Pillows					
Photos					
Clocks					
Plants					
Misc.					
Yearly Total					
5 Year Grand Total					

This chapter will explain how to give the eco-friendly touch to the room where you spend a full third of your time. For this reason, we need to take a closer look at things like the fabrics and carpeting we choose, the mattress and bedding we sleep on, and our choice of lighting.

Bedroom Lighting-Light up Your Love Life

For a bedroom, begin with a soft, low-level central light that illuminates the whole room as well as the corners. This can be anything from a basic overhead light to a dramatic pendant light that can be turned on and off at the door and by your bed, with the option of a dimmer switch to save electricity. Other options to consider are recessed down lights, built into the ceiling and largely hidden from sight as well as low-voltage spot lights, which are great for highlighting art work. Also, consider providing light for reading by choosing swing-arm, flexible bedside lamps or night stand table lamps. For closets, energy-efficient CFL's or fluorescent bulbs are especially useful so that you can color coordinate and put away your clothes easily. The main goal in bedroom lighting is to have healthy restful lighting that is never monotonous or glaring. This means there should be a variety of lights, but not so many as to create clutter and waste electricity.

Compact Fluorescent Light Bulbs
An Energy Saving Powerhouse

Recent developments in fluorescent light bulbs have been marvelous. Lasting up to thirteen times longer then standard incandescent light bulbs, the new types of fluorescent bulbs called compact fluorescent lighting (or CFL's), on average, use one quarter the electricity of regular incandescent bulbs, and thereby keep a power plant from emitting three quarters of a ton of carbon dioxide. Even though a CFL bulb requires a higher initial investment, in the long run the monetary and environmental savings more than make up that difference. You might especially appreciate the long life of CFL bulbs for those hard to reach places like high hallway ceilings-as they will help avoid frequent encounters with the stepladder! For this reason, these bulbs are also great for porch and other outdoor lighting systems. Compact fluorescents now come in all shapes and sizes to fit most fixtures.

How Can I Save Two Thousand Dollars?

Want to put two thousand dollars in the bank for a dream vacation or for your kids' college education? All you have to do is to replace every incandescent light bulb in your house with compact fluorescent light bulbs (CFLs). If you have an average size house of 1,500 square feet and use an average of 75 watts for each of forty-five light bulbs, after eight years, you will save well over two thousand dollars in energy costs. (Based on an average energy cost of $.08 kWh and each bulb saving $6.19 per year.)

But what about that flickering, pale ugly and sickly looking light that fluorescent light tubes are known for? Many people feel uncomfortable and agitated under the flickering glare of traditional fluorescent tubes. Do these CFL light bulbs have the same effect? The answer is no. First of all, they are now available in bulbs along with tubes, and they emit a much softer nonflickering light.

Natural and Synthetic Bedroom Fabrics
Cover yourself with Mother Nature's Finest.

Bedspreads, Blankets, and Bedding

Most of us sleep, dream and breathe in a room full of synthetics and chemically treated natural fabrics-all night, every night. These manmade fabrics off-gas an array of harmful chemicals plus they have an agricultural and manufacturing history that is not particularly positive for both humans and the environment.

Even though there is little evidence to link synthetic fibers like polyester, acrylic and nylon directly to major health problems, research shows that your skin can absorb the harmful chemicals they contain, which may include phenol, vinyl chloride, and plastics.[28] In addition, many cotton/poly or other synthetic fabrics are coated with formaldehyde to prevent wrinkling. Anything labeled as "crease-proof", "easy-care", "permanent press" or "waterproof" probably has been treated with formaldehyde. Also, many poly/cotton bed linen products are also coated with carcinogenic flame-retardants like TRIS. Although banned for use in children's sleepwear, it is still used on many textiles.[29]

It is also important to consider the impact of synthetics on the environment. Most synthetics are made of nonrenewable fossil fuels, create toxic by-products when manufactured and are not biodegradable or recyclable. If you find yourself losing enthusiasm for purchasing synthetics, read on.

In terms of personal comfort, synthetics fabrics that are used in the bedroom tend to be hot and clammy in warm weather, do not absorb moisture very well and are a breeding ground for bacteria. They also tend to be difficult to clean and require synthetically based polluting detergents to remove oil and other stains. Finally, most people find that synthetic fabrics are simply not as comfortable as natural fabrics.

Inside Story

One pair of jeans and a t-shirt uses one full pound of synthetic fertilizers and farm chemicals!

Cotton and the Environment?

For nearly four thousand years, cotton was grown organically- everywhere. After World War II, cotton became one of the most pesticide and fertilizer-intensive crops grown anywhere in the world. In 1997 alone, organic cotton textile companies eliminated the need for using 43,000 pounds of pesticides and 485,100 pounds of synthetic nitrogen fertilizer, all of which can end up in our soil, water, and elsewhere in the environment. If the world returned to growing cotton organically, it would reduce the world's overall pesticide use by a whopping twenty-five percent! Put another way, each pair of cotton jeans and t-shirt made from conventionally grown cotton, requires one whole pound of toxic chemicals.

In appearance, cotton fabrics look innocent enough- pure, simple, and comfortable; something you would wrap a newborn baby in. But you may not be aware of how many chemical and energy-intensive processes a cotton pillow has gone through before it finds its way to your bed. The list is long.

Cotton is considered the "universal fiber" because it can be found everywhere. Derived from the mallow family, cotton is a subtropical plant that has been harvested for thousands of years in Egypt, Asia and South America. There are many types of cotton species, but one of the most durable and comfortable is Egyptian cotton, which has the longest, strongest and silkiest fibers.

To get to the final product, most cotton now has anything but a simple processing history. While growing in the field, large amounts of fertilizer and pesticides are usually applied to the plants to kill boll weevils and pink boll worms. Unfortunately, since pests are becoming more and more resistant to these pesticides, newer and more toxic chemicals are constantly being applied.

When the cotton is mature, their bolls burst open and are ready to harvest. It is at this point that another chemical is often applied, a spray defoliant that causes the leaves to fall off, but leaves the bolls on the stems so that the picking equipment can harvest the cotton. Herbicide and flame jets may also be used at this point to kill other weeds in the field.

Once the cotton is picked, energy-intensive mechanical processes are used to clean the seeds and compress them into bales. Then, when at the mills, many other mechanical applications take place, which include boiling, bleaching with chlorine and mercerizing with a caustic soda. After even more treatment, most cotton cloth is dyed with synthetic dyes and treated with a host of other chemicals to make it wrinkle resistant, soil resistant, flame resistant, mildew resistant, rot resistant and/or water resistant. Sound appealing? Perhaps organic cotton is worth investigating after all.

Organic Cotton Fabrics - An Earthwise Breakthrough on the Horizon

Organic cotton has recently become widely available, making it possible for us to sleep on comforters, pillowcases, sheets, blankets and other bedroom products without having to breathe many toxic chemicals. To be sold as organic, cotton must be certified free of pesticides and insecticides for at least three years. Crop rotation, beneficial insects, and organic fertilizers and other sustainable farming methods are used in place of harsh chemicals.

Bedroom Linen Choices

Comforters, Duvet Covers, and Bedspreads
Price: $40 - $300

The most eco-friendly choices for comforters, bedspreads, and duvets are those made of certified organic cotton, silk, down/feathers and quilts made of reused fabrics. Keep in mind that it is always more eco-friendly to buy a duvet cover and use your old comforter as a filling rather than to buy a brand new comforter and thus waste more resources.

When shopping for a bed cover, it is best to get one with natural fiber stuffing like organic cotton or wool, which doesn't need to be dry-cleaned with harmful solvents. To reduce the number of times you have to clean your comforter, try using a comforter cover or protector and occasionally hang the comforter out in fresh, unpolluted air.

Blankets - Tuck Yourself in with Natural Warmth

Wool blankets untreated with chemical mothproofing are among the best choices for blankets. Since they "breathe," they are warm in the winter and cool in the summer, and come from an environmentally renewable source-sheep. If you store wool blankets in air tight, sealed containers or tightly closed plastic bags, and wash them before putting them away in storage, there is no need to purchase wool blankets treated with chemical moth repellent. The moth larva, which is what actually eats the fabric, is attracted to stains and dirty fabric. Also, try substituting cedar wood chips or herbal repellents for chemical mothballs, which may be intolerable for chemically sensitive individuals.

Organic cotton and "green" cotton are another good choice. Green cotton describes cotton that has been washed with natural-based soap, but not treated with other chemicals, except possibly natural dyes. Try to avoid poly/cotton mixes and other synthetics since they do not "breathe," are not very biodegradable and are composed of questionable chemicals. Purchase blankets that can be washed and dried at home; laundering protects against dust mites. If your blanket says, "dry clean only," ask your dry cleaner if they can clean it in a wet cleaning procedure without using carcinogenic toxic solvents.

Electric Blankets - Is this Your Best Choice for Keeping Warm?

In colder climates, many people have found electric blankets a cozy and tempting creature comfort. But, especially in older blankets, the wiring can produce what some scientists consider unhealthy levels of electromagnetic fields that have been potentially linked to various health ailments like brain tumors, leukemia and Alzheimer's disease. Other problems with electric blankets include the heating of synthetic fabric that can encourage chemical off-gassing and higher energy bills. In addition, these blankets require special care for cleaning so may not get cleaned as often.

Pillows - Lay Your Head on Feather Light Delight
Prices: Pillow Cases-$15-$45 each
Pillow Inserts-$10-$90 each

Down or feather are the best choices for pillows. Other good natural fiber choices are wool, buckwheat, unbleached kapok and natural rubber latex. Because they are used so close to your nose and mouth, try to stay away from synthetics or synthetic blends because they do not absorb moisture well and off-gas harmful chemicals. Natural latex pillows from Brazilian rubber trees are particularly ideal for people who are allergic to dust mites because dust mites can not survive well in this type of material. The only drawback is that natural rubber latex tends to get moldy in humid conditions.

Ergonomic pillows, commonly referred to as anatomical, butter-fly or neck roll pillows, especially if made of natural fabric, are another good choice. These are particularly helpful for people who suffer from neck, shoulder and back problems, since ergonomic pillows prevent the spine from twisting, which helps to avoid unnatural straining. For proper support, a pillow should be placed so that it is properly aligned with the rest of your body.

Sheets - Natural and Luxurious
Price: $15-$75 each

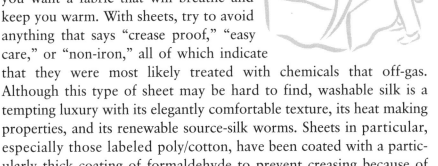

Organic or "green" cotton and silk are your best choices for sheets. Again, you want a fabric that will breathe and keep you warm. With sheets, try to avoid anything that says "crease proof," "easy care," or "non-iron," all of which indicate that they were most likely treated with chemicals that off-gas. Although this type of sheet may be hard to find, washable silk is a tempting luxury with its elegantly comfortable texture, its heat making properties, and its renewable source-silk worms. Sheets in particular, especially those labeled poly/cotton, have been coated with a partic-ularly thick coating of formaldehyde to prevent creasing because of their continuous use and frequent laundering. Washing sheets can reduce chemical emission levels, but will probably not remove them completely.

Mattresses - An Essential for a Good Night Sleep
Price: $300 - $3000+

Once upon a time, mattresses were simply cotton bags stuffed with wool, straw, cotton or rags. Later, they were improved by adding wooden frames with ropes stretched in between.

These days, mattresses are complex bedding mechanisms that are healthful in some ways but not in others. The good news is that high quality mattresses often offer an engineering design that keeps the spine straight, supports other parts of the body and prevents poor posture, as well as neck, shoulder and back problems. Less expensive mattresses often do not have these ergonomic features. The bad news is that many mattresses off-gas a variety of chemicals from their stain resistant, fire-retardant, synthetic foam, batting and covering materials. Whenever possible, try to find a mattress composed of natural fibers like wool, organic cotton, rubber or non-allergenic latex, and covered with a natural fiber mattress case. Natural fiber mattresses are superior to synthetics in the way that they breathe and absorb perspiration. This is a good thing since we perspire one liter of sweat as we sleep each night! If you have to have a synthetic-based mattress, you might want to cover it with a good densely woven barrier cloth to protect yourself from dust mites. To ensure yourself years of cushioning comfort and ergonomic support, research all the options before purchasing a mattress.

The first thing to ask when shopping for a mattress is if it will provide sufficient back support. Make sure that you choose an ergonomic mattress that will support your spine. When you are flat, the spine should form a shallow s-shape, and when you are on your side, a straight horizontal line.[30] This is much more important than how "cushy" or firm a mattress is, because if your spine is not straight, that discomfort will be with you wherever you go, awake or asleep. Of course, it is also important when shopping to select the mattress that feels most comfortable when you lie on it.

Also, make sure to flip your mattress every six months, and rotate it from head to toe six months after that. This will prevent the mattress from developing large depressions from where you have slept. Your bed should be a place of rest not one of strain.

Are Waterbeds Energy Hogs?

A waterbed is essentially a large vinyl bag. Vinyl can off-gas toxic chemicals like vinyl chloride and when the waterbed heater is turned up, the off-gassing increases. In addition, waterbeds usually offer little ergonomic support. Heated waterbeds will do anything but reduce your electricity bill. To heat the bed continuously, some waterbeds require up to 320 watts of energy per day. This is almost the equivalent of keeping three, 100 watt standing lamps turned on all day every day, or about as much energy as it takes to run a clothes dryer for one year!

Carpeting
Lush, Plush, and Earthwise

Americans discard 920 million square yards of carpeting per year.[31]

When it comes to carpets, retaining your existing carpeting is probably the most eco-friendly option since you are not consuming more resources. But there are other problems associated with carpeting, including dust mites, chemical off-gassing and cleaning. Most synthetic carpeting needs to be replaced every eight to fifteen years, while bamboo, cork and wood flooring can last a lifetime. If you have hardwood flooring, consider yourself lucky. You can make the most of hardwood flooring by adding a finish and/or an area rug. But if you like the warmth, insulation, noise control, and comfort of carpeting, read on.

The Delights of Wool Carpeting
Price: $25-$100+/sq. yd.

One of the most exciting possibilities for eco-friendly flooring is wool carpeting. Natural wool carpeting lasts three to four times longer than nylon or other synthetic carpeting, stays much cleaner than synthetic carpets, insulates the room well and has a much more luxurious look than synthetic rugs. Most wool now comes from New Zealand, where sheep graze naturally year round, making their wool coats extremely strong and durable. Their wool is usually washed three to four times to reduce the level of allergens. Another positive aspect of wool is that, once installed, it will not emit the harmful chemicals that synthetics can, which may cause low-grade headaches and fatigue. In fact, wool absorbs indoor contaminants while resisting dirt and soiling. Wool provides natural heat and sound insulation and is a natural flame retardant. It also resists static electricity.

When shopping for wool carpeting, try to find some with non-synthetic backing like jute, as synthetics are not biodegradable and often emit toxic off- gases. Expect to pay a little more for natural fibers. Remember, you get what you pay for. If you find wool carpeting out of your price range, consider a half wool, half synthetic blend, which is usually available for a much lower price. Although it may not be perfect, it will still provide many of wool's benefits. Wool carpets come in various styles: berbers, cut piles and loops. When purchasing wool, try to select a neutral color. This will give you greater flexibility when you want to make additional decorating changes and can be especially helpful if you eventually want to sell your house. Lime green or tangerine may not be what the buyer has in mind!

Recycled Synthetic Carpeting
Prices: Recycled polyester carpeting-$10-$27/sq. yd.
Conventional nylon carpeting-$20+/sq. yd.

Thirty six recycled plastic bottles yield one square yard of carpet [32]

If wool carpeting isn't your choice, and you still want wall-to-wall carpeting, one eco-friendly option is recycled polyester carpeting. Recycled- content carpet fibers are spun from recycled plastic drink containers and look just as attractive as traditional synthetic carpeting. They also are stain resistant and relatively inexpensive. When shopping for this type of carpeting, look for anything labeled "PET" which means that it is made from recycled materials. Most recycled carpeting is made up of polyesters. Try to avoid nylon, olefin or polypropylene carpeting, which are not usually made from recycled materials.

Many people who suffer from Multiple Chemical Sensitivity (MCS) or asthma have found carpeting to be one of the major home health hazards. One positive option when selecting synthetic or synthetic-blend carpeting is to find one that carries the Carpet and Rug

Institute's (CRI) "green label." This is a voluntary program in which participating manufacturers test their products for low chemical emissions. While this is a step in the right direction, this labeling system is limited and cannot yet guarantee these standards in all of its carpets.

How Can I Keep Carpet Pollution to a Minimum?

For many people who live in climates where it's often cold, or find the idea of cold bare floors less than inviting, the best option besides natural wool carpeting is to do everything possible to keep the carpeting as pollution-free and clean as possible. To begin with, when installing a carpet, ask the carpeting store to unroll the carpet for three to seven days in their warehouse to air out some of the chemical off-gases. (The highest emissions occur during the first three months after installation and gradually decline over time.) In the rare case that you are not installing carpet padding, ask the installers to use or provide them with solvent-free carpet adhesives such as Bio Shield's Natural Cork Adhesive #16 which can be purchased through the Eco Design Co. This is important, since carpet adhesives can release 10 to 100 times more toxic pollution than carpeting itself.

Whenever possible, use medium weight, natural carpet padding like wool or jute since it is low toxic and biodegradable. If you have to avoid natural padding altogether because of allergies, use recycled carpet padding instead. Sold under the name "rebond" carpet padding, this padding typically looks like a colorful patchwork. It is usually composed of discarded upholstery padding from the automotive, furniture and other industries.

After the carpet is laid, open as many windows and doors as possible, and use a portable fan to ventilate the house for at least one or two weeks after the installation. For this reason, it is probably a good idea to install carpeting during the warmer months so you can open the windows freely.

Once you have carpeting in your house, you'll want to keep it as clean as possible. Vacuum regularly with a specially filtered high efficiency particulate vacuum (or HEPA vacuum), or a central vacuum system that's vented to the outdoors. Regular vacuuming keeps dust, pollen and dust mite problems to a minimum. It's also a good idea to steam clean your carpet at least once or twice a year. One of the simplest and best solutions for keeping carpet clean is to have people remove their shoes before entering the house. Leave some heavy-duty wool socks by the door so that people always have something warm and durable to wear inside.

When it comes to taking care of carpet odors and spots, try these simple but effective methods. To absorb carpet odors, sprinkle the area with baking soda and vacuum. Small spots can be effectively removed with a club-soda solution and an absorbent sponge or cotton towel.

(Note: Before using one of these methods, test for color fastness on a hidden area of the carpet.)

Bedroom Furniture - **Refer to Living/Dining Room Chapter p. 97.**

Chapter 6

THE GARDEN

CREATE A NON-TOXIC GARDEN OASIS

For many, our garden is our favorite place to retreat. Few would deny the power of nature to renew, restore and bring back a sense of joy and peace. There are many ways we can enhance this experience through Earthwise product selections, which include deck and playground furniture, deck washes and finishes, roof treatments and other non-toxic yard products. This chapter also looks at the quintessential American lawn to see how eco-friendly it really is and suggests less resource-intensive care options. We'll also briefly cover water conservation, and what you can do if there is toxic lead in the soil.

This chapter can help you implement Earthwise maintenance techniques for the grounds surrounding your home. Many wonderful books already exist that can guide you through the nuances of ecological garden management. For a list of recommended books offering in-depth, Earth-friendly landscaping and organic gardening instructions, please refer to the appendix.

Playground Sets and Wood Decks
Avoid Toxic Wood Products

Research shows that 90 percent of wooden decks, play structures and picnic tables in the United States contain hazardous levels of arsenic, which according to the EPA, is a "known human carcinogen." Even structures that are up to fifteen years old still have high levels of arsenic near the surface of the wood and often contaminate the soil underneath. In fact, CCA lumber, (what much outdoor wood is called because it is treated with copper, chromium and arsenic to protect against insects and rot) is highly toxic. According to a recent EPA report, "one out of every 500 children who regularly plays on swing sets and decks made from arsenic-treated wood (or one child in an average-sized elementary school), will develop lung or bladder cancer in life as a result of these exposures."

What can you do to protect you and your family from CCA pressure-treated wood? First, make sure to purchase products made without CCA wood or that are made from metal, plastic or wood treated with arsenic and chromium-free ACQ (alkaline copper quat). If you are looking for a temporary solution, you can make CCA products safer by replacing parts like hand railings that come into skin contact with naturally rot-resistant cedar or redwood. You can also seal CCA products annually with a hard sealant like polyurethane, hard lacquer or a standard paint. If you have a deck, make sure you give it a standard deck treatment every six months. Cover CCA picnic tables with a non-porous tablecloth. Also, make sure children wash their hands after playing in a pressure-treated wooden play set or sand box, although it's probably not a good idea for them to be there in the first place. Fortunately, the Environmental Protection Agency is phasing out the use of arsenic in pressure-treated wood, thereby reducing the availability of CCA products in playgrounds and residences.

Another attractive, durable and eco-friendly alternative to CCA-treated wood is "composite decking" which goes by the brand names of Trex® Easy Care Decking®, or Nexwood®decking. These products are made from recycled plastic bags, plastic soda bottles, rice hulls and wood dust. These products save trees; contain no toxic chemicals or preservatives, will not splinter or rot, resist sunlight, moisture and insects and never need protective sealants or finishes. They come in a variety of standard lumber sizes and simulated wood grain colors and surfaces that are designed to increase traction.

Afraid that composite decking may not look "natural" enough? Well, consider this. They look good enough for many national parks, including the Grand Canyon and the Everglades. Composite decking can also be found at Disney World and perhaps even at your local supermarket.

Outdoor Furniture

When selecting deck or patio furniture, consider a set made from certified or plantation-grown wood. Better yet, buy something locally made that supports your local community and does not use large amounts of energy to transport.

If possible, try refurbishing your existing furniture with a new coat of water-based, low-VOC exterior paint, or search for a unique find at a garage sale or antique store. Another option is getting furniture made from composite materials or recycled plastic.

Deck Washes

If you are like many people who read the latest and greatest about organic gardening, you may have come across comments about using cleaners, sealers, and finishes that are environmentally non-toxic. But when you go to the home improvement store, the product choices are overwhelming; few of which, claim to be Earthwise. What does one do?

Here are some options for making your purchasing experience a little more user-friendly. For washing mold, algae and muck off your deck after a long cold winter, hydrogen peroxide-based cleaners are your best bet. Unlike chlorine, hydrogen peroxide-based cleaners break down quickly into water and oxygen and do little harm to the environment.

Other options include organic biodegradable products like Safer® Moss and Algae Cleaner and Worry Free® Moss and Algae Control by Lilly Miller.

Keep in mind that even though pressure washing is a relatively Earthwise way of cleaning your deck and roof, it can damage some types of wooden roof shingles.

Deck Finishes

Before applying any finish, make sure the deck is thoroughly cleaned and sanded so that once the finish is applied it will have a clean, smooth look and last a long time. If you suspect your wood is pressure-treated, wear a mask while sanding to protect yourself from CCA toxicity. (Pressure-treated wood usually has staple-sized indentations in it).

Now that your deck is clean, what kind of finish won't harm your plants, soil or the neighboring watershed? Choose a finish made from organic plant oils, or protect your newly cleaned and sanded deck with a water-based outdoor paint or sealant that contains an ultraviolet (UV) protective additive to help it weather the elements.

Avoid traditional deck stains and sealants that emit highly flammable, air-polluting vapors. This includes products that contain toxic solvents like toluene and xylene, which when inhaled can cause respiratory problems and/or effect the brain and nervous system. Why work with these nasty chemicals when there are much better alternatives like Timber-Tek UV Deck Finish?

Roof Treatments

How can we keep our roofs and home exteriors clean without having a toxic chemical impact on our local streams?

Handy Dandy Roof Treatment Tips

It's the end of the winter. As the sun peeks through the clouds for the first time in months, you notice an ugly, green algae slime all over the exterior of your home. How do you remove it without using harsh chemicals that wind up in your soil and the neighborhood watershed? For a gentle impact, follow these tips:

1) An ounce of prevention is worth a pound of cure. Keep debris and leaves, which hold moisture and promote fungal growth and damage, off your roof.
2) Minimize your use of chemicals containing the following: copper, zinc and iron sulfate metals.
3) Treat roofs only in dry weather to allow the treatment to soak into the roof.
4) Use the smallest concentration possible as indicated on the product label.
5) Disconnect the down spouts from gutters when applying liquid treatment. That way, the run-off will filter through the soil and break down instead of going directly into the nearest stream.
6) When looking for a roof treatment professional, ask how they usually handle run-off and what types of chemicals they use. Examples of eco-friendly roof treatments that are also deck washes are Safer® Moss and Algae Cleaner or Worry Free® Moss and Algae Controls by Lilly Miller.
7) Next time you replace your roof, choose a non-organic roofing material that resists moss and algae growth.

Pressure Washing
Take the Toxic Pressure off Your Local Streams

When pressure-washing your home, deck, driveway or car, try these tips to prevent pollutants from entering storm drains and ditches that lead to waterways.

Handy Dandy Pressure Washing Tips

1) If you wash your car at home, park it on grass to allow pollutants to filter through the soil.
2) Direct the spray toward a grassy or planted area.
3) Instead of using water, sweep sidewalks and driveways, and put the sweepings in the garbage to keep pollutants and litter out of the watershed.
4) Before pressure-washing, make sure to remove paint flakes, grease and other pollutants that will wash into waterways; especially lead paint that is poisonous to children, animals and plants.
5) If you feel you need to use a cleaner, try this less toxic recipe:

Low-Toxic Pressure Washing Cleaning Recipe
- Two cups of mild laundry detergent
- 1/2 cup of vinegar
- 1/4 cup of lemon juice
You may not even need to use this cleaner often. Pressure washing alone removes most dirt and grime.

Lead in the Soil

Soil and dust are sources of lead exposure especially if children play in it. Lead usually enters soil from deteriorating or improperly removed lead-based paint, industrial emissions from sources like lead battery plants and smelters or emissions from leaded gasoline. Although gasoline sold in the U.S. no longer contains lead, the soil next to roads may still contain high lead levels since lead doesn't break down.

Refer to p. 24 about the health effects of lead.

Handy Dandy Lead Soil Tips

What can you do if you discover a high lead presence in your soil? Here are some options:

1) Cover the soil with grass, gravel or stones. (Make sure children or pets can't disturb it.)
2) Have a certified lead removal contractor remove the soil.
3) Make sure children wash their hands after playing outside in an area that may contain lead.
4) Remove shoes before entering your home, especially if it contains carpeting.
5) Plant your garden in a lead-free area away from busy roads and painted buildings.
6) Make sure that your child's sand box doesn't contain lead-contaminated sand.
7) Wash your child's toys often.
8) Contact your local lead abatement specialist for further testing and clean-up options.

Barbecue Grills-The All-American Appliance

Barbecuing is an American institution. How can you barbecue in the most eco-friendly way possible? Although it uses a non-renewable fuel resource, a gas grill is preferable to a charcoal grill. Charcoal typically produces more pollution and less heat.

When shopping for the perfect grill, look for something that is durable and not larger than you really need to avoid using excess fuel, space and resources - including those in your wallet! Try getting a grill with two burner controls, since those burn more evenly and efficiently than just one. If you need to use charcoal, look for a brand that is made of hardwood and has no additives in it. For lighting coal, use a chimney starter.

Your Natural/Organic Garden Shopping List

For many, an ideal garden is a sanctuary that blends in harmoniously with the neighborhood and natural community. It is a place where beautiful plants, birds and insects thrive; a place free from pesticides and chemical fertilizers: a place where chemical runoff doesn't harm local streams and rivers.

Use this list when shopping for garden products to determine whether a product is really eco-friendly.

Handy Dandy Earthwise Garden Products

Soil amendments and fertilizers-
-coconut peat (a peat moss alternative)
-cocoa mulch
-cover crops
-manure
-compost
-worm castings

Weed control-
-weed block fabrics
-lawn alternatives (eco-lawn, wildflowers, native plants, shrubs etc.)
-soap-based herbicides
-pre-emergent corn gluten
-boiling water

Handy Dandy Tips cont.

Fertilizers-
-alfalfa meal
-blood meal
-bone meal
-cottonseed meal (pesticide-free)
-feather meal
-fish (liquid or dry)
-kelp or kelp meal
-oyster shell
-soybean meal
-rock phosphate

Physical Controls-
-confusion lure (pheromone)
-copper slug barriers
-floating row covers
-pheromone traps
-sticky barriers (e.g., tangle foot)
-sticky insect traps
-yellow jacket traps
-other garden pest insect traps
-Slug-Go or Oscar-Go

Minerals-
-copper fungicide
-lime sulfur
-sulfur fungicide
-Bordeaux mix

Handy Dandy Tips cont.

Soaps, dusts, and oils-
-boric acid baits (for ants and cockroaches)
-diatomaceous earth
-fish oil
-insecticide soap
-summer oil
-neem oil
-sapodilla dust

Other-
-bird houses
-bird baths
-compost bins
-hot pepper wax
-mole repellents
-predator urines
-red worms (for composting)
-worm bins
-hazel nut shells (pebble path substitute)

Make Your Garden Stream-Friendly

Most people are not aware that what they do in their gardens may have a direct impact on their local streams and rivers, especially when rain washes toxins into local waterways. By carefully monitoring lawns and gardens, and by being careful about what we build, we can do our best to keep waterways clean, healthy and bountiful for both wildlife and ourselves. This will help provide wildlife a healthy habitat, prevent floods, and ensure that we have clean drinking water.

Handy Dandy Stream-Friendly Garden Tips

Here's what we all can do to help:
1) Plant native plants. They usually require less water, fertilizer and pesticides than their non-native cousins do. By planting perennials, you will be able to enjoy watching these plants grow each successive year. On the other hand, annuals die off each year and need to be replaced, costing more money and resources in the end.
2) Minimize the use of pesticides and chemical fertilizers. Instead, opt for slow-releasing organic fertilizer, organic farming and pesticide alternatives.
3) Minimize your use of pavement, keeping driveways and walkways as small as possible. Also, use bark or gravel for driveways and paths.
4) Direct gutters to areas where the water can seep slowly into the soil, and away from pavement, streams and septic drain fields.
5) Clean up after your pet, keeping pet waste off paved areas and away from streams.
6) Avoid pouring household chemicals, pesticides, grease, soapy water and car oil down storm drains, which are often connected directly to streams. Call your local city or county information line for the nearest toxic waste disposal site.
7) Use non-toxic and biodegradable household cleaners, especially if you have a septic tank.
8) Sweep driveways and sidewalks instead of hosing them down.
9) Recycle or compost yard debris.
10) Go to car washes that recycle their water.
11) Prevent erosion and runoff with shrubs, rock gardens and ground water.

Handy Dandy Tips cont.

12) Consider reducing or replacing your lawn with more natural landscaping like shrubs, trees, ground cover and native plants that needs less water, fertilizers and herbicides.
13) Keep bark dust away from pavement, ditches and storm drains where it can potentially wash away, clog storm drains and contribute to flooding.

Tips for Garden Water Conservation

Water means life. It is what sets the Earth apart from every other planet. But only three percent of the Earth's water is fresh and the demand for fresh water is growing.

Garden Water Conservation–
**The average person's outside daily water use.
(For homes with landscapes)**
Lawn and Shrubs-68 gallons (85%)
Garden-8 gallons (10%)
Car Washing-4 gallons (5%)[33]

A well-watered garden can consume up to 80% of a household's daily water usage. At a time when more and more people are sharing an ever-shrinking supply of water, follow these tips to make your garden more Earthwise.

Handy Dandy Water Conservation Tips

1) Install a drip system. Drip systems can save up to 70 percent of water otherwise used in a garden, by directing the water to the specific plants that need it, in the amounts they need. Consider adding a timer to prevent over watering. Soaker hoses also conserve water by directing water flow to where it is needed.

2) Water only in the morning and evening, giving your plants only what they need. Excess water running down the driveway is a sign that you are over-watering your plants. A garden hose left running for an hour can waste up to 300 gallons of water!

3) Condition your soil for water retention. Consider adding compost, manure and coconut mulch to your garden beds. This added organic matter acts like a sponge in the garden, helping to retain water, while giving plants the nutrition they need. Organic compost also helps to loosen heavy clay soils and gives body to sandy soils so that it can retain nutrients and moisture longer.

4) Use mulch- By spreading a 2"- 4" layer of mulch in your garden beds, you will discourage weeds and reduce water lost through evaporation.

5) Water deeply and less often- By watering deeply, you allow water to seep into the ground so less will evaporate. This also helps plants develop a stronger root system, enabling them to go longer without water.

Lawns - How to Make Yours River-Friendly

Lawns have become part of the American dream. They also can be an environmental menace requiring excessive resources to maintain, and are one of the top sources of pollution to local streams and rivers.

If you want to keep your lawn largely free of disease, weeds and insect pests, consider setting up a preventative lawn health care program. Ongoing pest problems are usually a sign that your lawn is not getting what it needs to stay healthy and that your lawn eco-system is not balanced. How can you maintain a lovely lawn while having as little environmental impact as possible? Here are some tips.

Handy Dandy Lawn Tips

Fertilizing Your Lawn-Don't be Overly Generous.

If you are going to fertilize your lawn, consider doing it only once a year in the late spring with a slow-releasing organic fertilizer. Non-organic synthetic fertilizers contain chemicals that are more likely to run off into waterways since they are not immediately absorbed by plants. This runoff leads to algae blooms, or eutrophication of neighboring watersheds. Algae blooms can also suffocate aquatic life and lead to dead zones where most life has ceased to exist. Aquatic dead zones have increased in size and number with the proliferation of synthetic fertilizer use.

Water and Mow Your Lawn Infrequently

When watering your lawn, water deeply but infrequently. Your lawn only needs to be watered when it begins to wilt from dryness. You can tell when it needs water if the color dulls and footprints stay in the grass for more than a few seconds. When you do water, water deeply, and then avoid watering for a while to encourage deeper roots that can withstand the pressure of drought.

If you water too often, you run the risk of disease and the possibility of losing precious nutrients, soil, fertilizer and water due to excessive runoff.

Save Your Grass Clippings

If you want to reduce your need for lawn fertilizer by 50 percent, leave your grass clippings on the lawn after mowing. They will disintegrate and slowly release nutrients back into the lawn and create a layer of mulch for retaining water.

Aerate and Compost Your Lawn

Another way to improve your lawn is to aerate it and top-dress it with fine compost, about a quarter of an inch deep. The way to aerate a lawn in the late spring and fall is to push a garden fork six inches deep every four inches into the lawn and work back and forth to loosen the soil. You can also rent a power aerator to do more of the work for you. By aerating your lawn and spreading a thin layer of compost over it, you will have a thicker, healthier lawn that will help discourage weeds. The compost fertilizes the soil, helps your lawn retain moisture in the summer and aids in preventing erosion.

Prevent a Thatch Build Up

Thatch is the build up of dead grass material between the lawn and the soil. When thatch gets deeper than 3/4 of an inch, water and nutrients have a hard time reaching the roots. When shopping for grass seed, avoid strains that are more prone to thatch build-up. And avoid using chemical fertilizers that can contribute to a heavy layer of thatch.

Choose the Right Grass Strain and Mow less Frequently

When selecting grass seed, make sure you select the right strain for your region. For instance, if you live in a hot and dry climate, don't choose a strain that needs a lot of water.

There is no need to mow frequently. If you let your grass grow to 2.5 to 3.5 inches, you will be saving energy and weeds will have a harder time growing. Also, keep in mind that gas-powered lawn movers can be very polluting.

One hour of gas-powered mowing equals the amount of
pollution created by driving 100 miles in an average size car.[34]

Avoid Lawn Herbicides

Weeds have less of a chance to thrive if you keep your lawn soil healthy. Avoid using "weed and feed" products. The pesticides in "weed and feed" products damage your soil quality by killing beneficial microorganisms and insects. There is also evidence that pesticides can harm humans, pets, wildlife and neighboring watersheds. Why spread weed killer over your entire lawn if you just want to get rid of a few weeds? Either learn to embrace the sight of a few weeds in your lawn, pull them out by hand in the spring and fall when the soil is moist, or use a mower to keep them under control. But if the sight of weeds makes you crazy, one method for killing weeds is to use boiling water. Make it a habit of going outside to pour boiling water left over from cooking.

Resources

Handy Dandy Tips

17 Ways to Save Money in Eco-Home Improvement

1) Use slipcovers instead of buying a new sofa or chair.
2) Use compact fluorescent bulbs (CFL's) instead of regular incandescent bulbs.
3) Make cleaning products out of vinegar and water.
4) Refinish your floors instead of buying new flooring.
5) Buy carpet made from recycled bottles.
6) Refinish your kitchen instead of replacing it.
7) Buy antiques and vintage furniture instead of new furniture.
8) Buy energy and water efficient appliances.
9) Install a garden drip system.
10) Use cloth napkins and kitchen towels instead of paper ones.
11) Install eco-friendly landscaping.
12) Buy energy efficient honeycomb window shades.
13) Refurbish furniture, floors and cabinets instead of buying new ones.
14) Dry your clothes on a drying rack instead of in a dryer.
15) Cover up floor blemishes with an area rug.
16) Use cold water when washing clothes and dishes.
17) Instead of heating the whole house, use a space heater to heat up just the room you are using.

SOURCES

Natural Capitalism by Paul Hawken, Amory Lovins and L. Hunter Lovins. New York, New York: Little, Brown and Company, 1999, 322 pp.

The Home Decorator's Bible by Anoop Parikh, Deborah Robertson, Thomas Lane, Elizabeth Hilliard and Melanie Paine. New York, New York: Crown Publishers, Inc., 1996, 345 pp.

Nontoxic, Natural, and Earthwise by Debra Dadd. Los Angeles, California: Jeremy P. Tarcher, Inc., 1991, 316 pp.

The New Natural House Book by David Pearson. New York, New York: Simon and Schuster, 1998, 288 pp.

Affluenza by John De Graaf, David Wann and Thomas H. Naylor. San Francisco, California: Berrett-Koehler Publishers, Inc., 2001, 268 pp.

If You Love This Planet by Helen Caldicott, M.D. New York, New York: W.W. Norton and Company, 1992, 203 pp.

This Place on Earth by Alan T. Durning. Seattle, Washington: Sasquatch Books, 1996, 310 pp.

Eco-Renovation by Edward Harland. Post Mills, Vermont: Chelsea Green Publishing Company, 1993, 252 pp.

Room Redux by Joann Eckstut and Sheran James. San Francisco, California: Chronicle Books, 1999, 248 pp.

Materials and Components of Interior Architecture by J. Rosemary Riggs. Upper Saddle River, New Jersey: Prentice Hall, 2003, 216 pp.

Mary Gilliatt's Interior Design Course by Mary Gilliat. New York, New York: Watson-Guptil Publications, 2001, 206 pp.

Seven Layers of Interior Design by Christopher Lowell. New York, New York: Discovery Books, 2000, 170 pp.

Inside Today's Home by LuAnn Nissen, Ray Faulkner and Sarah Faulkner. Reno, Nevada: Wadsworth Thomson Learning, 1994, 650 pp.

Healthy Home by Jill Blake. New York, New York: Watson-Guptill Publications, 1998, 181 pp.

The Healthy Home by Linda Mason Hunter. New York, New York: Simon and Schuster, Inc., 1990, 294 pp.

Lighten Up! - A Practical Guide to Residential Lighting by Randall Whitehead. San Francisco, California: Randall Whitehead Lighting, Inc., 2003, 177 pp.

The Healthy Household by Lynn Marie Bower. Bloomington, IN: The Healthy House Institute, 1995, 480 pp.

The Healthy House: How to Buy One, How to Build One, How to Cure a "Sick" One by John Bower. Bloomington, IN: The Healthy House Institute, Third Edition, 1997, 672 pp.

Creating a Healthy Household by Lynn Marie Bower. Bloomington, IN: The Healthy House Institute, 1995, 657 pp.

Natural Decorating by Elizabeth Wilhide and Joanna Copestick. New York, New York: Abbeville Press, 1995, 139 pp.

Eco Chic by Rebecca Tanqueray. London, England: Carlton Books, 2000, 141 pp.

Book of Home Design Techniques by Nicholas Springman and Jane Chapman. Alexandria, Virginia: Time-Life Books, 2001, 245 pp.

Kitchens by Chris Casson Madden. New York, New York: Clarkson Potter Publishers, 1993, 278 pp.

Colors of Living Kitchens by Jill Pilaroscia. Rockport, Massachusetts: Rockport Publishers, Inc., 1995, 105 pp.

Decorating 1-2-3 by Home Depot. Des Moines, IA: Meredith Books, 2000, 409 pp.

The Healthy Home Kit by Ingrid Ritchie, PhD. Dearborn Financial Publishing, Inc., 1995, 373 pp.

FOOTNOTES

1   Paul Hawkin, Amory Lovins and Hunter Lovins, *Natural Capitalism*. New York: Little, Brown and Company, 1999. pp. 51-52

2   Paul Hawkin, Amory Lovins and Hunter Lovins, *Natural Capitalism*. New York: Little, Brown and Company, 1999. pp. 51-52

3   Paul Hawkin, Amory Lovins and Hunter Lovins, *Natural Capitalism*. New York: Little, Brown and Company, 1999. pp. 51-52

4   Durning, Alan. *This Place on Earth*. Seattle: Sasquatch Books. 1996. pp. 132

5   Durning, Alan. *This Place on Earth*. Seattle: Sasquatch Books. 1996. pp. 159

6   Caldicott, Helen, M.D. *If You Love This Planet*. New York: W.W. Norton and Company, 1992. pp. 70

7   Durning, Alan. *This Place on Earth*. Seattle: Sasquatch Books. 1996. pp. 159

8   Caldicott, Helen, M.D. *If You Love This Planet*. New York: W.W. Norton and Company, 1992. pp. 66

9   Durning, Alan. *This Place on Earth*. Seattle: Sasquatch Books. 1996. pp. 132

10 Ligon, Linda. "Stroke of Brilliance." *Natural Home* May-June 2001: pp. 61

11 Ligon, Linda. "Stroke of Brilliance." *Natural Home* May-June 2001: pp. 61

12 Cowley, Geoffrey. "Getting the Lead Out." *Newsweek* Feb. 2003: 52-55

13 Cowley, Geoffrey. "Getting the Lead Out." *Newsweek* Feb. 2003: 52-55

14 Dadd, Debra. *Nontoxic, Natural & Earthwise*. Los Angeles: Jeremy P. Tarcher, Inc., 1990. pp. 43

15   Dadd, Debra. *Nontoxic, Natural, & Earthwise.* Los Angeles: Jeremy
     P. Tarcher, Inc., 1990. pp. 47

16   "Water Whiz Quiz." *Natural Home* July-Aug. 2003: pp. 24

17   "Five Plastic Bottles Equals One Ski Jacket," *Organic Style* Jan-Feb.
     2003: pp. 27

18   Bongiorno, Lori. " Our Reproductive Health: What are the Risks?"
     Green Guide Jan-Feb. 2004: pp. 2

19   "Nuts and Bolts." *Natural Home* Jan-Feb. 2003: pp. 78

20   Caldicott, Helen, M.D. *If You Love This Planet.* New York: W.W.
     Norton and Company, 1992. pp. 67

21   Dadd, Debra. *Nontoxic, Natural, & Earthwise.* Los Angeles: Jeremy
     P. Tarcher, Inc., 1990. pp. 140

22   Paul Hawkin, Amory Lovins and Hunter Lovins, *Natural
     Capitalism.* New York: Little, Brown and Company, 1999. pp. 105

23   Paul Hawkin, Amory Lovins and Hunter Lovins, *Natural
     Capitalism.* New York: Little, Brown and Company, 1999. pp. 52

24   Ritchie, Ingrid PhD. *The Healthy Home Kit.* Dearborn Financial
     Publishing, Inc., 1995. pp. 115

25   Hunter, Linda. *The Healthy Home.* New York: Simon & Schuster,
     1989. pp. 77

26   Hunter, Linda. *The Healthy Home.* New York: Simon & Schuster,
     1989. pp. 75

27   Hunter, Linda. *The Healthy Home.* New York: Simon & Schuster,
     1989. pp. 77

28   Dadd, Debra. *Nontoxic, Natural, & Earthwise.* Los Angeles: Jeremy
     P. Tarcher, Inc., 1990. pp. 219

29   Dadd, Debra. *Nontoxic, Natural, & Earthwise.* Los Angeles: Jeremy
     P. Tarcher, Inc., 1990. pp. 220

30 Pearson, David. *The New Natural House Book.* New York: Simon & Schuster, 1998. pp. 213

31 Paul Hawkin, Amory Lovins and Hunter Lovins, *Natural Capitalism.* New York: Little, Brown and Company, 1999. pp. 52

32 Wolf, Anastasia. " Called on Carpet." *Natural Home* Jan-Feb. 2003: pp. 72

33 Dadd, Debra. *Nontoxic, Natural, & Earthwise.* Los Angeles: Jeremy P. Tarcher, Inc., 1990. pp. 46

34 "Dirty Little Secret." *Natural Home* July-Aug. 2003: pp. 25

About the Author
Kristina Detjen

Kristina's goal is to help make your living environment a place where you can thrive and feel inspired-all the while being gentle on the Earth. She has been an interior design consultant for eight years, studying as an honor student at the Heritage School of Design, Portland Community College, and the University of Colorado. Kristina has also written articles, appeared on TV, and has lectured about eco-friendly interior design and home improvement. Her clients include the historic Marina Motel in San Francisco which was featured in Sunset Magazine. As a fourth- generation descendent of a San Franciso "gold rush" mining family, Kristina's extensive travels throughout the world have broadened her sense of style and increased her understanding of a wide variety of cultures, which she integrates into her work.

Appendix

ORGANIC GARDENING BOOKS

The Organic Gardening Book by Geoff Hamilton. New York,
New York: DK Publishing, Inc, 1993, 288 pp.

Gardening for the Future of the Earth by Howard-Yana Shapiro, PH.D.
and John Harrison. New York, New York: Bantam Books, 2000,
224 pp.

The Natural Garden Book by Peter Harper. New York, New York:
Simon and Schuster Inc., 1994, 287 pp.

Edible Landscaping by Rosalind Creasy. San Francisco, Ca: Sierra Club
Books, 1982, 379 pp.

Easy-Care Perennial Gardens by Susan McClure. Emmaus,
Pennsylvania: Rodale Press, Inc., 1997, 160 pp.

Bringing the Garden to Life by Carol Williams. New York, New York:
Bantam Books, 1998, 271 pp.

Index

compact fluorescent light (CFL)
bulbs, 30, 106, 126–127
compact fluorescent strips, 45
composite decking, 141
compost, 151, 153
concrete countertops, 27, 32
concrete flooring, 34, 53–54
concrete mixture countertops, 34
convection ovens, 44, 68
cookware, 63–66
Corian™, 51
cork flooring
characteristics of, 89
cost of, 27, 34, 44, 85
uses for, 51–52
Corningware®, 66
costs
appliances, 44, 68
art work, 81, 107, 123
cabinets, 107
carpeting, 84, 107, 123
countertops, 27, 32, 44
fireplace insert, natural gas, 119
flooring, 27, 34–35, 44, 52, 85
furniture, 107, 123–124
lighting, 27, 43, 82, 107, 123
mirrors, 107, 123
paint, 21, 27, 43, 82, 107, 124
rugs, 85, 107
tile, 44
wallpaper, 27, 43, 82, 107, 124
window treatments, 27, 43, 82, 107, 124
cotton, conventionally grown, 29, 129
cotton, organic, 129, 130–131, 132, 133
cotton/polyester fabrics, 128, 129
coughing, 91
countertops, 32–34, 49–51
crease-proof fabrics, 128

CRI (Carpet and Rug Institute), 136–137
Crystal Aire, 92, 95
Crystal Shield, 92
curtain rods, installation, 119
cutting boards, 60, 67

D
deck finishes and washes, 141–142
decorating style, 11–25, 29
defoliants, 129
design theme, 11–25, 29
dining rooms, 81–82, 97–99, 107, 108
dinnerware, 66–67
dioxin, 55
dishwashers, 44, 68–69
disinfectants, 60, 61
dizziness, 22, 62, 94
down pillows, 132
draperies, 117–119
drinking water
automatic dispensers, 70
chilled, 79
filters for, 40, 71
lead contamination in, 40–41
dry cleaning, 132
dryers, 44, 68, 73–74
Durat™, 44, 51
dust mites, 132, 134, 135, 138
dusts, for the garden, 148
duvet covers, 131
dyes, in rugs, 96

E
Easy Care Decking®, 141
easy-care fabrics, 128
eclectic look, 12
Egyptian cotton, 129
electric blankets, 132
electric dryers, 73–74
electric stoves, 74–75

ORDER FORM
for additional copies of
The Earthwise Home Manual

Detach and mail this form with your check
or your credit card number.

Please send me_____ copies @ **$15.95**
plus **$2.00** for shipping one copy, plus **$1.00** for
each additional copy to the same address.

❑   Check enclosed
❑   Charge my credit card
❑   VISA   ❑   Mastercard

Card Number   _____
Expiration date _____
Signature   _____

Name   _____
Address _____
City _____
State_____ Zip _____
Email   _____

❑ Mail to above address   ❑ Different address
            Please provide:

_____

_____

Total books ____ plus ____ for shipping = _____

For more than 10 copies call: 503-760-6678
or contact our website at
www.greenhomepublishing.com

Mail to: Green Home Publishing
P.O Box 82335, Portland, OR 97282-0335